W9-CXK-615

SAT* CHEMISTRY SUBJECT TEST

CRASH COURSE™

Vivek Peri

By Adrian Dingle

The Westminster Schools
Atlanta, Georgia

Research & Education Association
Visit our website at: www.rea.com

Planet Friendly Publishing
✔ Made in the United States
✔ Printed on Recycled Paper
    Text: 10%   Cover: 10%
Learn more: www.greenedition.org

GREEN
EDITION ®

At REA we're committed to producing books in an Earth-friendly manner and to helping our customers make greener choices.

Manufacturing books in the United States ensures compliance with strict environmental laws and eliminates the need for international freight shipping, a major contributor to global air pollution.

And printing on recycled paper helps minimize our consumption of trees, water and fossil fuels. This book was printed on paper made with **10% post-consumer waste**. According to the Environmental Paper Network's Paper Calculator, by using this innovative paper instead of conventional papers, we achieved the following environmental benefits:

**Trees Saved: 4 • Air Emissions Eliminated: 751 pounds
Water Saved: 681 gallons • Solid Waste Eliminated: 221 pounds**

Courier Corporation, the manufacturer of this book, owns the Green Edition Trademark.
For more information on our environmental practices, please visit us online at **www.rea.com/green**

Research & Education Association
61 Ethel Road West
Piscataway, New Jersey 08854
E-mail: info@rea.com

SAT CHEMISTRY SUBJECT TEST CRASH COURSE™

Printed in the United States of America

Library of Congress Control Number 2012932837

ISBN-13: 978-0-7386-1034-4
ISBN-10: 0-7386-1034-8

Cover image Robert Daly/OJO Images/Getty Images

All trademarks cited in this publication are the property of their respective owners.

Crash Course™ and REA® are trademarks of Research & Education Association, Inc.

SAT CHEMISTRY SUBJECT TEST CRASH COURSE™
TABLE OF CONTENTS

PART III

States of Matter

PART IV

Reaction Types

Stoichiometry

PART V

Equilibrium and Reaction Rates

PART VI

Thermochemistry

PART VII

Descriptive Chemistry

PART VIII

PART IX

Laboratory

ONLINE PRACTICE EXAM........... *www.rea.com/studycenter*

ABOUT THIS BOOK

REA's *SAT Chemistry Subject Test Crash Course* is the first book of its kind for the last-minute studier or any student who wants a quick refresher on the subject. The book will provide you with an accurate and complete representation of the SAT Chemistry Subject Test.

Written by an expert whose professional focus over the last 22 years has been preparing students for standardized tests, our easy-to-read format gives students a crash course in chemistry. The targeted review chapters prepare students for the exam by focusing on the important topics that will mostly likely be addressed on the SAT Chemistry Subject Test.

Unlike other test preps, REA's *SAT Chemistry Crash Course* gives you a review specifically focused on what you really need to study in order to ace the exam. The review chapters offer you a concise way to learn all the important facts, terms, and key topics before the exam.

The introduction discusses the keys to your success on the SAT Subject Test in Chemistry and shows you strategies to help build your overall score. Also included is an introduction to the three different types of questions—classification, relationship analysis, and five-choice completion—you will encounter on the SAT Chemistry Subject Test.

The remaining parts of the text make up our review chapters. Each chapter presents the essential information you need to know about chemistry. Interspersed throughout the review chapters are Test Tips written to help you attain the highest score on the SAT Chemistry Subject Test.

To check your test readiness for the SAT Chemistry exam, either before or after studying this Crash Course, take our **FREE online practice exam**. To access your free practice exam, visit *www.rea.com/studycenter* and follow the on-screen instructions. This true-to-format test features automatic scoring, and detailed explanations of all answers, which will help you identify your strengths and weaknesses so you'll be ready on exam day!

No matter how or when you prepare for the SAT Chemistry Subject Test, REA's *Crash Course* will show you how to study efficiently and strategically, so you can boost your score.

Good luck on your SAT Chemistry Subject Test!

ABOUT OUR AUTHOR

Adrian Dingle is a chemistry educator and author, with a total of 22 years of experience teaching in the United States and the United Kingdom. He is the creator of the award-winning chemistry website, *www.adriandingleschemistrypages.com.*

The focus of his teaching career has been on preparing students for standardized tests, AP and SAT subject tests in the United States, with an emphasis on A2/AS levels in the United Kingdom, and International Baccalaureate in both countries. An Englishman, he lives in Atlanta, Georgia, where he teaches at The Westminster Schools. He holds a B.Sc. (Hons.) Chemistry, and a Postgraduate Certificate in Education, both from the University of Exeter in England.

His other books include *The Periodic Table: Elements With Style* and *How To Make A Universe With 92 Ingredients*, the School Library Association of the UK's Information Book Award winner for 2011, and the winner, in 2012, of the prestigious literary prize *Wissenschaftsbuch des Jahre,* which is sponsored by the Austrian Ministry of Science and Research.

ACKNOWLEDGMENTS

In addition to our author, we would like to thank Larry B. Kling, Vice President, Editorial, for his overall guidance, which brought this publication to completion; Pam Weston, Publisher, for setting the quality standards for production integrity and managing the publication to completion; Alice Leonard, Senior Editor, for editorial project management; and Diane Goldschmidt, Managing Editor, for preflight editorial review.

We also extend our special thanks to S4Carlisle Publishing Services for content development and typesetting this edition.

PART I:

INTRODUCTION

KEYS TO SUCCESS ON THE SAT CHEMISTRY SUBJECT TEST

BACKGROUND

The SAT Chemistry Subject Test assesses the knowledge and understanding that one might reasonably expect to have gained after successfully completing a one-year, college preparatory chemistry course in high school.

It is assumed that a laboratory component will have been included in the course because some of the questions on the test will examine knowledge and understanding of the equipment and techniques employed in typical high school chemistry lab situations.

Rudimentary mathematical skills associated with the metric system, algebra, ratios, direct and inverse proportions, the use of exponents, and scientific notation is also part of the student's anticipated knowledge base.

Chemistry-related skills that are anticipated include recall, application, and synthesis of knowledge in approximately 20%, 45%, and 35% of the test, respectively.

LOGISTICS

The test is 1 hour in length, and consists of 85 multiple-choice questions.

You are provided with a periodic table of the elements that will be useful in many questions on the test, including those that ask about subatomic particles (protons, neutrons, and electrons), stoichiometry, periodicity and periodic patterns, plus many other areas. Expect to refer to it a lot.

You may not use a calculator, but the lack of access to a calculator does not mean that calculations are excluded from the test, only that they will be relatively simple and that you should be able to solve them without electronic help.

QUESTIONS

The test is divided into three parts (A, B, and C), but you may move about among the sections of the test as you please.

Part A—Classification Questions

The classification questions comprise approximately 20–25 questions on the test. In these questions, a set of five answers is given, and you must match these choices to the numbered statements that immediately follow. You may use each choice once, more than once, or not at all in each case. See the following example.

Questions 1–3 refer to the following molecules:

(A) CO_2 (D) CO

(B) NH_3 (E) H_2O

(C) CH_4

1. Contains three bonding pairs of electrons and only one nonbonding (lone) pair in its Lewis diagram.

 Answer (B). The Lewis diagram for ammonia (NH_3) has a total of 8 electrons. Those electrons form 3 covalent bonds between the central nitrogen atom and the 3 terminal hydrogen atoms and a lone pair of electrons sits on the nitrogen atom in order to fulfill its octet.

2. Is tetrahedral in shape.

Answer (C). VSEPR predicts that a tetrahedral shape will be formed when 4 bonding pairs and 0 lone pairs are present around the central atom in a Lewis diagram. Methane (CH_4) has 4 bonding pairs and 0 lone pairs and is therefore tetrahedral.

3. Contains at least one double bond.

 Answer (A). The Lewis structure for carbon dioxide (CO_2) shows each oxygen atom bonded to the central carbon atom with a double bond. This structure satisfies all octets using a total of 16 electrons.

Part B—Relationship Analysis Questions

The relationship analysis questions comprise 15 questions on the test. In these questions two statements or assertions are made. In order to answer the question, you must make three decisions. First, is statement I true or false? Second, is statement II true or false? Third, is statement II a *correct explanation* (CE) of statement I? You will only need to make the final decision if you find that both statements I and II are true. See the following examples.

Examples of Relationship Analysis Questions

I		II
101. Fluorine F_2, is a good reducing agent	because	fluorine is a member of a group commonly known as the halogens.
102. The reaction of zinc metal with 0.1 M sulfuric acid leads to the formation of a gas	because	sulfuric acid produces carbon dioxide when reacted with zinc metal.
103. A 0.1 M solution of hydrochloric acid is considered to be a strong acid	because	HCl is 100% dissociated when in aqueous solution.

The questions are answered on a special section of the answer sheet labeled "Chemistry" and start with question number 101 using a grid similar to the following example.

Examples of Answer Grid for Relationship Analysis Questions

	I	II	Correct Explanation
101.	T● ○F	●T ○F	○
102.	○T ●F	T● ○F	○
103.	○T ●F	○T ●F	●

Part C—Five-Choice Completion Questions

The five-choice completion questions comprise approximately 45–50 questions on the test. In these questions incomplete statements or questions are posed and then five answer choices are given. In this part you may also see questions where several correct answers are given and you are asked to select the one *inappropriate* solution. These questions usually contain a word in capital letters such as NOT, LEAST or EXCEPT. For example:

1. All of the following molecules are correctly paired with their atom geometries, EXCEPT

   (A) CH_4, tetrahedral
   (B) NH_3, trigonal pyramidal
   (C) H_2O, linear
   (D) CO_2, linear
   (E) CO, linear

2. Which of the following solids would one expect to have a color other than white?

   (A) NaCl (D) $Mg(NO_3)_2$
   (B) KCl (E) $KMnO_4$
   (C) $NaNO_3$

   The five-choice completion questions also include a certain type of question where multiple, potentially correct answers are offered (usually three or four), and you must choose the correct combination of answers. For example:

3. Which of the following is a reasonable and accurate representation of Boyle's law when applied to gases?

   I. $P_1V_1 = P_2V_2$
   II. At constant temperature with a fixed mass of gas, pressure and volume are inversely proportional.
   III. When keeping n and T constant, an increase in pressure of a gas will result in a decrease in volume.

   (A) I only (D) I and III only
   (B) III only (E) I, II, and III
   (C) I and II only

CONTENT

The test is divided into eight broad topic areas, with each of those broken down further into more specific objectives. Each topic has more or less emphasis depending upon the extent to which it is examined on the test. The main ideas and their relative importance are summarized in the following table.

Topic Areas and Approximate Percentage of Questions on the SAT Chemistry Test

Structure of Matter (25%)	States of Matter (16%)
Atomic structure (and experimental evidence)	*Gases*
Quantum numbers	*Liquids and Solids*
Electronic configuration	*Phase changes and phase diagrams*
Periodic trends	*Solutions (molarity, % by mass,*
Lewis structures and shape	*preparation, stoichiometry,*
Ionic, covalent, and metallic bonding	*solubility, colligative properties)*
Intermolecular forces and polarity	

(continued)

Topic Areas and Approximate Percentage of Questions on the SAT Chemistry Test (*continued*)

Reaction Types (14%)

Acids and bases (Brønsted-Lowry,
    strength, pH, titrations, indicators)
REDOX (combustion, oxidation
    numbers, activity series)
Precipitation

Stoichiometry (14%)

Moles (Avogadro's number, empirical
    formula, molecular formula)
Chemical equations (balancing*,
    stoichiometry, % yield, limiting
    reactant)

Descriptive Chemistry (12%)

Nomenclature
Periodic trends
Reactivity and prediction
    of products*
Simple organic compounds
Compounds of environmental
    concern

Laboratory (8%)

Laboratory equipment
Measurements
Procedures
Observations
Safety
Calculations
Data analysis (interpretations
    of graphical data)
Conclusions from observations

Equilibrium and Reaction Rates (5%)

Le Chatelier's principle
Equilibrium constants
Equilibrium expressions
Rates of reaction (factors effecting
    rate, potential energy diagrams,
    activation energy)

Thermochemistry (6%)

Conservation of energy
Calorimetry
Specific heat
Enthalpy associated with phase change
Enthalpy associated with chemical
    reactions
Heating and cooling curves
Entropy

---

*Approximately five questions on every edition of the test are related to balancing and/or predicting products of chemical reactions and are distributed among the various topic areas.

   Bear the following quote from the College Board in mind when considering the content you have learned in your chemistry course, and the content that you may find on the SAT test.

   "Please note that this test reflects what is commonly taught in high school. Due to differences in high school classes, it's likely that most students will find questions on topics they're not familiar with. This is nothing to worry about. You do not have to get every question correct to receive the highest score (800) for the test. Many students do well despite not having studied every topic covered."

SCORING

The test is scored by awarding 1 point for each correct answer and subtracting one quarter of 1 point for each wrong answer to produce a raw score. Questions that are left blank (or ones where more than one answer is selected) are ignored and carry no penalty. The raw scores (which can range from −21 to +85) are converted to a scaled score that ranges from 200 to 800. Each time the test is administered, it is possible that slightly different scaled scores will be generated from the same raw score. This is to ensure that the relative ease (or difficulty) of each test is taken into account, and to attempt to ensure that the scaled score on the test remains consistent, regardless of the particular version of the test that the student takes. The following is a typical conversion table.

SAT Chemistry Score Conversion Table*

Raw Score	Scaled Score	Raw Score	Scaled Score	Raw Score	Scaled Score
85	800	70	760	55	670
84	800	69	750	54	670
83	800	68	750	53	660
82	800	67	740	52	660
81	800	66	730	51	650
80	800	65	730	50	650
79	800	64	720	49	640
78	800	63	720	48	640
77	790	62	710	47	630
76	790	61	710	46	620
75	780	60	700	45	620
74	780	59	700	44	610
73	770	58	690	43	610
72	770	57	690	42	600
71	760	56	680	41	600

(continued)

SAT Chemistry Score Conversion Table* (*continued*)

Raw Score	Scaled Score	Raw Score	Scaled Score	Raw Score	Scaled Score
40	590	20	480	0	370
39	590	19	480	−1	370
38	580	18	470	−2	360
37	580	17	470	−3	360
36	570	16	460	−4	350
35	560	15	450	−5	340
34	560	14	450	−6	340
33	550	13	440	−7	330
32	550	12	440	−8	330
31	540	11	430	−9	320
30	540	10	430	−10	320
29	530	9	420	−11	310
28	530	8	420	−12	310
27	520	7	410	−13	300
26	510	6	410	−14	300
25	510	5	400	−15	290
24	500	4	390	−16	280
23	500	3	390	−17	280
22	490	2	380	−18	270
21	490	1	380	−20	270

*Scoring for REA's practice tests strongly approximates that for the actual test. Bear in mind that scaled scores for different editions of the SAT Chemistry test are adjusted to take into account small shifts in content and in the overall performance of the test-taker population.

HINTS AND TIPS FOR TAKING THE TEST

As in all tests and exams, the key to attaining the highest scores on the SAT Chemistry Subject Test boils down to two simple things. First, knowing *what* can be assessed, and second, knowing *how* that content is assessed. This book gives a targeted breakdown of the material that you can reasonably expect to be assessed on the SAT Subject Test in Chemistry. The combination of knowing what can (and importantly what cannot) be asked will lead to a streamlined attack on the business of succeeding on the test.

The first step is to familiarize yourself with pure nuts and bolts (the logistics) of the exam, which have been covered earlier in this chapter. Knowing the type and number of questions that will appear, plus the format of the test, will help a great deal in both relieving stress and removing the unknown.

Working steadily through all of the questions is very important. You must keep an eye on the time, and you must get to the end of the test. It could be that the last few questions on the test are ones that you know how to answer, so by not reaching that point in the test you would be doing yourself a disservice. Glance up every 10 minutes to see if you have completed a multiple of approximately 15 questions, i.e., after 10 minutes you should have done approximately 15 questions, after 20 minutes, approximately 30 questions, and so on. This will keep you focused and moving through the test and will help you to avoid getting stuck on any particular question.

The one resource that you have access to during the test that is not in your head, is the periodic table. Use it! The periodic table will be useful in many areas of the test so make sure that you remember that it can help.

Remember that it is not necessary to answer every question on the test. You can leave some answers blank. You can also employ a targeted guessing strategy, which becomes more effective as you eliminate wrong answers from the choices available. However, be careful. One sure way to get a question wrong is to eliminate the correct answer and then guess from the remaining choices! If you really cannot identify and eliminate an answer that you know to be wrong, then that is a question that is a good candidate to be left blank.

PART II:
STRUCTURE OF MATTER

ATOMIC STRUCTURE: EXPERIMENTAL EVIDENCE FOR ATOMIC STRUCTURE

I. ATOMIC THEORY—THOUGHTS ON THE STRUCTURE AND NATURE OF THE ATOM SPAN MANY CENTURIES

A. EARLY IDEAS

1. Circa 400–5 BCE. Greek philosopher Democritus proposes the idea of matter being comprised of small, indivisible particles (*atomos*).
2. Late 18th Century. Lavoisier proposes the law of conservation of mass, i.e., that matter cannot be created or destroyed. Proust proposes the law of definite proportions (or the law of constant composition), i.e., that a given compound will always contain the same proportion of chemical elements by mass.

B. DALTON'S ATOMIC THEORY

1. In the early 19th century, using the previously somewhat unconnected ideas discussed earlier, Englishman John Dalton formulated his atomic theory.
   i. Matter is composed of tiny particles called *atoms*.
   ii. All atoms of a given element are identical.
   iii. The atoms of a given element are different from those of any other given element.
   iv. Atoms of different elements combine in small, whole number ratios to form compounds. A given compound always has the same relative numbers and types of atoms (law of definite proportions), but different compounds containing the same elements can be formed, by combining elements in differing small whole number ratios (the law of

multiple proportions). For example, 12 g of carbon can combine with 16 g of oxygen to form carbon monoxide, CO, but 12 grams of carbon can also combine with 32 g of oxygen to form carbon dioxide, CO_2. The ratio of oxygen masses that combine with 12 g of carbon is 16:32, i.e., 1:2, a simple, whole number ratio.

v. Atoms cannot be created or destroyed in a chemical reaction—they are simply rearranged to form new substances (law of conservation of mass).

C. EXPERIMENTAL EVIDENCE FOR THE ATOMIC MODEL

1. Several experiments were being carried out, and ideas formulated, in the late 19th and early 20th centuries that began to identify the subatomic particles that comprise the atom along with their position and nature.

Summary of Early Experiments Used to Formulate Atomic Theory

Scientist	Experiment	Knowledge Gained	Relating To
Crookes (Late 19th century)	Cathode ray tube	Negative particles of some kind exist	Electron
J. J. Thomson (circa 1900)	Cathode ray deflection	Mass: charge ratio of the electron determined	Electron
Millikan (1908)	Oil drop experiment	Charge on the electron	Electron
Rutherford, Marsden, and Geiger (1909)	Gold foil experiment	Nucleus with positive charge present in atom	The nucleus of an atom and the proton
Chadwick (1932)	Possible existence of neutron	Particles with no charge exist in atom's nucleus	Neutron

2. In the very early 1900s, the plum-pudding model (electrons dispersed in a "pudding" of positive charge) was the working model.

D. MODERN VIEW OF THE ATOM

1. Niels Bohr took some of Rutherford's ideas and proposed the idea that the atom was comprised of a dense nucleus containing protons and neutrons that was being orbited by the electrons in specific, allowed orbits. Sometimes called the *solar system model*, the atom was then thought of as:

   i. A dense, central nucleus containing protons with a charge of +1, and a mass of 1 amu, and neutrons with a charge of 0 and a mass of 1 amu (amu = atomic mass unit).

   ii. Electrons with a charge of −1 and a mass of approx. 1/2,000 amu that are widely dispersed in specific positions outside of the nucleus. See the following diagram.

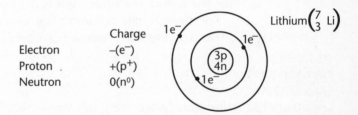

2. Schrödinger, de Broglie, and Heisenberg introduced wave functions and quantum mechanics to account for the fact that electrons exhibit properties that are associated with waves as well as being particles.

II. SYMBOLS, ATOMIC NUMBERS, MASS NUMBERS, AND ISOTOPES

A. EACH ELEMENT HAS A ONE- OR TWO-LETTER SYMBOL ON THE PERIODIC TABLE, AND TWO NUMBERS ASSOCIATED WITH IT (E.G., CARBON CAN BE DEPICTED AS $^6C_{12}$). THE SMALLER NUMBER IS CALLED THE *ATOMIC NUMBER* AND THE LARGER THE *MASS NUMBER*

1. Atomic number (Z) = the number of protons (positive particles) in the nucleus of one atom of that element. Because all atoms are neutral (carry no electrical charge), it also tells us the number of electrons (negative particles) in the atom.

2. Mass number (A) = number of protons + number of neutrons (neutral particles).

3. Isotopes. The number of protons and neutrons in atoms are always whole numbers, and as such one might expect the mass number to always be an integer, too. However, many elements have mass numbers recorded on the periodic table as noninteger values. Why?

   i. Atoms of the same element are defined by the number of protons that they contain; for example, atoms of carbon always have 6 protons and atoms of oxygen always have 8, and so on.

   ii. The number of neutrons present can vary and hence the mass numbers of the same element can vary, too.

   iii. Atoms of the same element with different numbers of neutrons are called *isotopes*.

   iv. The reported atomic mass is the average mass of all of the naturally occurring isotopes of an element, and so the mass number can be a noninteger value.

Example question:

Chromium has four naturally occurring isotopes—50, 52, 53, and 54—in abundances of 4.350%, 83.79%, 9.500%, and 2.360%, respectively. What is the average atomic mass of chromium?

(A) 48.06

(B) 50.06

(C) 52.06

(D) 54.06

(E) 55.06

Answer: (C)

The detailed calculation is (50*0.04350) + (52*0.8379) + (53*0.09500) + (54*0.02360) = 52.06.

Test Tip

This is a good example of a question that should remind you of two things:

1. No calculators are allowed on the test, so you will need to be able to do some simple, mental arithmetic and use estimation.

2. You should check all of your numerical answers to see if they make sense.

In the case of average atomic masses, the correct answer must be somewhere between the highest and the lowest isotopic mass, and must be closest to the most abundant isotope. Answers that do not fulfill these criteria do not make sense and you should think again.

Applying this simple, "Does it make sense?" test to all other numeric answers on the test will help you to identify any silly mistakes.

III. IONS

A. ATOMS BECOME IONS WHEN THEY CEASE TO BE NEUTRAL AND BECOME CHARGED BY EITHER LOSING OR GAINING ELECTRONS

1. Electrons are either removed from, or added to, the *valence shell* of that atom, i.e., the shell that is furthest from the nucleus.

2. Cations are positive and are formed by losing electrons, e.g., when an Na atom (11 protons, 11 electrons) loses an electron to become an Na^+ ion (11 protons, 10 electrons).

3. Anions are negative and are formed by gaining electrons, e.g., when an S atom (16 protons, 16 electrons) gains 2 electrons to become an S^{2-} ion (16 protons, 18 electrons).

Test Tip

The history behind the discovery of subatomic particles and the development of atomic theory is generally not examined heavily on the test. Because of this, you should focus your study and review on knowing the subatomic particles, their position and nature, and understanding isotopes and ions. Do not be concerned with a history lesson where a collection of dates and scientists' names need to be learned. However, you should be familiar with the broad ideas behind the development of atomic theory.

QUANTUM NUMBERS AND ENERGY LEVELS (ORBITALS)

I. **QUANTUM NUMBERS**

A. **FOUR QUANTUM NUMBERS ARE USED TO IDENTIFY THE SPECIFIC POSITION AND TYPE OF ELECTRON IN AN ATOM**

1. Schrödinger, de Broglie, and Heisenberg
    i. Following Bohr's development of the atomic model, the wavelike properties of electrons were incorporated (via quantum mechanics), by Schrödinger, de Broglie, and Heisenberg. This allowed predictions to be made about the specific positions of the electrons within the atom.
    ii. Electrons are found in very specific, quantized, three-dimensional spaces (called *orbitals*) around the atom, and these spaces are defined by wave functions that are mathematical solutions to the Schrödinger equation.
    iii. Each three-dimensional space is a probability map of where one might expect to find an electron and can be thought of as a "cloud."
    iv. The *Heisenberg uncertainty principle* states that the position and momentum of an electron can never be simultaneously, exactly known.
    v. Each of these three-dimensional spaces (orbitals) is located at a particular distance (or level) from the nucleus. The levels have increasing energy as one moves away from the nucleus.
    vi. The electronic structure of an atom can be described by the use of four *quantum numbers* which, when taken together, describe the specific

position of an electron in any given level of any given atom.

a) *Principal quantum number (n).* Each level (or shell) has a principal quantum number. The first shell has a quantum number of 1, the second shell a quantum number of 2, and so on. In each shell, the maximum number of electrons is given by $2(n^2)$. Using this, we can find the maximum number of electrons in each of the first four shells.

Maximum Number of Electrons in Each Quantum Shell

Shell and Principal Quantum Number (n)	Maximum Number of Electrons
1	2
2	8
3	18
4	32

b) *Azimuthal (or orbital angular momentum) quantum number (l).* Each shell is further divided into subshells. The number of subshells within any level is equal to the principal quantum number and the subshells are numbered with consecutive whole numbers starting from zero. In addition to the numbering system, the subshells are given the letters s, p, d, and f corresponding to the azimuthal numbers 0, 1, 2, and 3, respectively. The different types of subshell have different three-dimensional shapes: s orbitals are spherical, p orbitals are dumb-bell ("figure-eight") shaped and align themselves on x, y, and z axes, and d and f orbitals have more complicated shapes.

Summary of Azimuthal (Orbital Angular Momentum) Quantum Numbers

Shell and Principal Quantum Number (n)	Subshells and Azimuthal (Orbital Angular Momentum) Quantum Numbers (l)	Corresponding Letter
1	0	s
2	0, 1	s, p
3	0, 1, 2	s, p, d
4	0, 1, 2, 3	s, p, d, f

c) *Magnetic quantum number (m_l).* Each subshell is further divided into individual orbitals. The number of orbitals that are possible in each subshell is equal to twice the azimuthal quantum number plus one ($2l + 1$). Each orbital is given a number called the *magnetic quantum number*. Possible values of the magnetic quantum number are integer values from $-l$ to $+l$, including zero.

d) *Spin quantum number (m_s).* Each orbital can hold a maximum of two electrons. The *Pauli exclusion principle* states that no one electron can have exactly the same set of quantum numbers, so, because each orbital can hold a maximum of two electrons that would have the same set of the first three quantum numbers, it is the spin quantum number that allows distinction between them. It can have a value of $+\frac{1}{2}$ or $-\frac{1}{2}$.

Test Tip

The Pauli exclusion principle refers only to two electrons in the same atom and as such does NOT prevent two electrons in DIFFERENT atoms from having the same set of four quantum numbers. Do not be confused!

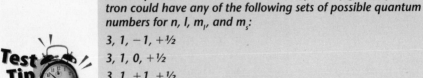

An electron in a given orbital may have a number of possible sets of quantum numbers, so, for example, any given 3p electron could have any of the following sets of possible quantum numbers for n, l, m_l, and m_s:

3, 1, −1, +½

3, 1, 0, +½

3, 1, +1, +½

3, 1, −1, −½

3, 1, 0, −½

3, 1, +1, −½

As such, questions about quantum numbers have the potential to use a phrase such as "a possible set of quantum numbers."

vii. Following is a summary of quantum possible numbers, shell and subshell designations, and their electrons.

Summary of Quantum Numbers

Principal Quantum Number (n)	Azimuthal Quantum Number (l)	Subshell Designation	Magnetic Quantum Numbers (m_l)	Number of Orbitals in Subshell and the Orbital Name	Maximum Number of Electrons in Subshell	Maximum Number of Electrons in Principal Shell
1	0	1s	0	1(1s)	2	2
2	0	2s	0	1(2s)	2	8
	1	2p	$-1, 0, +1$	3(2px, 2py, 2pz)	6	
3	0	3s	0	1(3s)	2	18
	1	3p	$-1, 0, +1$	3(3px, 3py, 3pz)	6	
	2	3d	$-2, -1, 0, +1, +2$	5(3dxy, 3dxz, $3dx^2-y^2$, 3dyz, $3dz^2$)	10	
4	0	4s	0	1(4s)	2	32
	1	4p	$-1, 0, +1$	3(4px, 4py, 4pz)	6	
	2	4d	$-2, -1, 0, +1, +2$	5(4dxy, 4dxz, $4dx^2-y^2$, 4dyz, $4dz^2$)	10	
	3	4f	$-3, -2, -1, 0, +1, +2, +3$	7(Various names)	14	

ELECTRON CONFIGURATIONS

I. RULES FOR FILLING ORBITALS (AUFBAU PRINCIPLE)

A. ELECTRON CONFIGURATIONS ARE DETERMINED ACCORDING TO A SPECIFIC SET OF RULES

1. Determine the number of electrons by referring to the atomic number of the atom.
2. Consider any charges caused by the loss or gain of electrons (i.e., consider whether you are dealing with ions).
   i. Elements and ions can be *isoelectronic* with one another, meaning that they have the same electronic configurations; for example, Mg^{2+} and Ne (both have 10 electrons) and S^{2-} and Ar (both have 18 electrons).
3. Lowest energy orbitals are filled first.
4. Orbitals have increasing energies, with 1s having the lowest energy, 2s the next, and so on.
   i. There is a minor complication here. The 4s orbital has a slightly lower energy than the 3d orbitals and as a result the 4s orbital is filled before the 3d orbitals. Similarly, the 5s orbital has a slightly lower energy than the 4d orbitals and as a result the 5s orbital is filled before the 4d orbitals. So, when filling the d orbitals, subtract one from the principal quantum number to determine the correct shell.

II. DETERMINING ELECTRONIC CONFIGURATION USING THE PERIODIC TABLE

A. THE PERIODIC TABLE CAN BE USED TO DETERMINE ELECTRONIC CONFIGURATION

1. The period number and block letter show the shell (principal quantum) number and type of electron, respectively. See the following diagram.

1s			
2s			2p
3s			3p
4s		3d	4p
5s		4d	5p
6s		5d	6p
7s		6d	
	4f		
	5f		

s block—Group 1 and 2
p block—Groups 13 through 18
d block—transition metals
f block—lanthanoid and actinoid

By far the easiest way to remember the sequence of orbital filling is by using the periodic table. Label the rows in the table with period numbers and the blocks with the letters p, d, and f. Remember to subtract 1 from the period number when entering the d block, and to subtract 2 from the period number when entering the f block, and to re-establish the period number when entering the p block.

2. Add 1 electron for each element until the orbital, then the subshell, and ultimately the whole shell, is full.

3. Record the electronic configuration in the format of *principal quantum number (shell), type of orbital,* and *number of electrons* (as a superscript). For example:

   i. Hydrogen has 1 electron that is found in the s orbital in the first shell; therefore, $1s^1$ (pronounced "one s one").

ii. Helium has 2 electrons that are found in the s orbital in the first shell; therefore, *1s²* (pronounced "one s two").

iii. Other examples: Starting at hydrogen each time, follow the periodic table to "build up" the electronic configurations shown in the following table.

Examples of Electronic Configurations

Element	# of Electrons	Electronic Configuration
F	9	$1s^2\ 2s^2\ 2p^5$
P	15	$1s^2\ 2s^2\ 2p^6\ 3s^2\ 3p^3$
Sb	51	$1s^2\ 2s^2\ 2p^6\ 3s^2\ 3p^6\ 4s^2$ $3d^{10}\ 4p^6\ 5s^2\ 4d^{10}\ 5p^3$

Test Tip

By adding the superscripts, you can calculate the total number of electrons in any given electronic configuration. This can serve as a useful check of your work.

4. There are anomalies when it comes to Cr and Cu. A half-filled or completely filled d shell is considered to have extra stability. Therefore, Cr and Cu have electronic configurations ending $4s^1\ 3d^5$ and $4s^1\ 3d^{10}$ rather than $4s^2$ $3d^4$ and $4s^2\ 3d^9$, respectively. In each case, one of the 4s electrons is promoted to the 3d shell to create a more stable electronic configuration.

5. The noble gas core method is used to abbreviate electronic configurations. Write the previous noble gas in square brackets and then fill orbitals as before; for example, because the noble gas prior to phosphorus in the periodic table is neon, its electronic configuration can be written as $[Ne]\ 3s^2\ 3p^3$.

6. The orbital diagram notation uses boxes to represent the orbitals and arrows to represent electrons. For example, see the following diagram.

Element	Electron Configuration	Orbital Diagram
H	$1s^1$	1s: ↑
He	$1s^2$	1s: ↑↓
Li	$1s^2 2s^1$	1s: ↑↓ 2s: ↑
Be	$1s^2 2s^2$	1s: ↑↓ 2s: ↑↓
B	$1s^2 2s^2 2p^1$	1s: ↑↓ 2s: ↑↓ 2p: ↑ □ □
C	$1s^2 2s^2 2p^2$	1s: ↑↓ 2s: ↑↓ 2p: ↑ ↑ □
N	$1s^2 2s^2 2p^3$	1s: ↑↓ 2s: ↑↓ 2p: ↑ ↑ ↑

    i. The *Pauli exclusion principle* is illustrated with electrons in the same orbital shown with opposite spins.

7. As you can see in the preceding diagram, the three 2p orbitals avoid having electrons paired until it is absolutely necessary. This is called *Hund's rule of maximum multiplicity* and it states that if there is more than one orbital with the same energy (degenerate), then 1 electron is placed into each orbital before any pairing takes place. All similar orbitals have a similar energy; for example, all three 2p orbitals have the same energy.

8. Depending on the circumstances, and what you are trying to illustrate, electronic configurations can be represented in a number of different ways; for example, nitrogen (7 electrons) can be represented as follows, each one showing different degrees of detail and having a different emphasis.

   i. $1s^2\ 2s^2\ 2p^3$

  ii. $1s^2\ 2s^2\ 2px^1\ 2py^1\ 2pz^1$

 iii. $[He]\ 2s^2\ 2p^3$

 iv. $[He]\ 2s^2\ 2px^1\ 2py^1\ 2pz^1$

9. An *excited state* is said to exist when an electron is promoted to a higher energy level than you might otherwise expect. The expected electronic configuration (lowest energy) is described as the *ground state*. For example, Mg in the ground state is $1s^2\ 2s^2\ 2p^6\ 3s^2$, but in an excited state, it could be $1s^2\ 2s^2\ 2p^6\ 3s^1\ 3p^1$.

PERIODIC TRENDS

I. PERIODICITY

A. A REGULAR, REPEATABLE PATTERN OF PROPERTIES IS OBSERVED WITHIN THE PERIODIC TABLE

1. Elements are arranged in the periodic table in order of ascending atomic number.

2. With ascending atomic number, a regular change in the outermost (valence) electronic configuration is observed.

3. In turn, with the regular change in valence electronic configuration, a regular variation of properties is also observed. This called the *periodic law or periodicity*.

4. A vertical column of elements is called a *group*. There are 18 groups on the periodic table numbered 1–18 from left to right. Elements in the same group have the same valence electronic configuration, so they have similar properties to one another.

   i. "s block" elements (valence electrons enter the s orbitals) are groups 1 and 2. Group 1 is comprised of elements that are collectively called the *alkali metals,* and group 2 is comprised of the *alkaline earth metals.*

   a) Group 1 elements are very reactive, soft metals; form 1+ ions; will liberate hydrogen from water and form basic (hydroxide) solutions; and have increasing reactivity as you move down the group.

   b) Group 2 elements are less reactive than group 1; are harder metals; form 2+ ions; will liberate hydrogen from water or steam; and form basic (hydroxide) solutions.

ii. "d block" elements (electrons enter the d orbitals) are groups 3 through 12. These groups are collectively known as the *transition metals*. Although, in reality, there is a subtle difference between the definitions of "d block" and "transition metal."

    a) Transition metals have multiple (positive) charges on their ions; often form brightly colored ions; can form complex ions (coordination compounds); are often used as catalysts; and have higher melting points and hardness than the metals in groups 1 and 2.

iii. "p block" elements (valence electrons enter the p orbitals) are groups 13 through 18. Some of these groups have common, collective names; others do not. Groups 13, 14, 15, and 16 are often simply called the *boron, carbon, nitrogen*, and *oxygen* groups respectively, but group 15 is sometimes called *the pnictogens* and group 16 is sometimes called *the chalcogens*. Groups 17 and 18 have very common collective names: *the halogens* (group 17) and *the noble gases* (group 18).

    a) Group 13 is headed by B, a nonmetal, but other group members are metals. They form 3+ ions, and Al is the most abundant metal in the earth's crust.

    b) Group 14 is headed by C, a nonmetal, followed by Si and Ge (semimetals), and through to Sn and Pb (metals). Semimetals are often used as semiconductors. The elements in this group are a mixture of nonmetals, semimetals, and metals—therefore, their properties can be variable. Sn and Pb form 2+ and 4+ ions.

    c) Group 15 is headed by N, a nonmetal, followed by P (another nonmetal), then As and Sb (semimetals) through to Bi (metal). The elements in this group are a mixture of nonmetals, semimetals, and metals—therefore, their properties can be variable. Nitrogen comprises approximately 78% of air. Elements in this group form 3− ions most commonly.

d) Group 16 is headed by O, a nonmetal, followed by S and Se (also nonmetals) through to Te and Po (semimetals). The elements in this group are a mixture of nonmetals and semimetals—therefore, their properties can be variable. Oxygen comprises approximately 21% of air and is essential to life. Elements in this group form 2− ions most commonly. Many sulfur compounds are responsible for bad smells.

e) Group 17 elements exist as diatomic molecules. The elements form 1− ions. Gases (F_2, Cl_2), a liquid (Br_2), and a solid (I_2) are all represented. Reactivity decreases as you move down the group.

f) Group 18 elements are unreactive because they have filled s and p subshells and as a result form very few compounds. This group is comprised of all gases.

The SAT Chemistry exam will sometimes start with a few questions that could be described as random factoids. For example, asking which metal is the most abundant in the earth's crust, which elements are used as semiconductors, which elements comprise air, or which element is responsible for unpleasant aromas. These are facts that would not necessarily be taught during a normal high school chemistry course, so try to read around the subject as much as you can to pick up the odd, interesting piece of trivia. It COULD mean an extra point or two on the test.

iv. "f block" elements (electrons enter the f orbitals) are placed at the bottom of the periodic table and are called the *lanthanoids* and *actinoids,* respectively. The f block includes many radioactive isotopes.

5. A horizontal row of elements is called a *period.*

   i. Elements in the same period have the same number of occupied electron shells.

   ii. Periods 1, 2, and 3 are sometimes called the *short periods.*

II. METALS, NONMETALS, AND SEMIMETALS (METALLOIDS)

A. ELEMENTS IN THE PERIODIC TABLE CAN BE BROADLY SORTED INTO THREE CATEGORIES, AS SHOWN IN THE FOLLOWING DIAGRAM

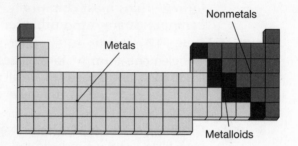

1. Metals
   - i. Most of the elements on the periodic table are metals.
   - ii. Metals are good conductors of heat.
   - iii. Metals are good conductors of electricity.
   - iv. Metals have luster (are shiny).
   - v. Metals are malleable (can be shaped) and ductile (can be drawn into thin wires).
2. Nonmetals
   - i. Nonmetals are found in the top right-hand corner of the periodic table.
   - ii. Nonmetals are generally poor conductors of heat and electricity.
   - iii. Nonmetals are brittle and dull.
3. Semimetals (Metalloids)
   - i. Semimetals are found on the "staircase" between the metals and nonmetals on the periodic table.
   - ii. In some circumstances, semimetals may act as metals, and other times they may act as nonmetals.

IONIZATION ENERGY

A. IONIZATION ENERGY IS THE ENERGY REQUIRED TO REMOVE ELECTRONS

1. *First ionization energy* is defined as the energy required to remove 1 mole of electrons from 1 mole of gaseous atoms to produce 1 mole of gaseous ions.

$$M_{(g)} \rightarrow M^+{}_{(g)} + e^-$$

2. *Second ionization energy* is defined as the energy change accompanying the following process.

$$M^+{}_{(g)} \rightarrow M^{2+}{}_{(g)} + e^-$$

3. Ionization energies are measured in units of kJ mol^{-1}. They have positive (endothermic) values indicating that energy must be "put in" in order to remove electrons.

4. The following are factors that affect the magnitude of the ionization energy. The attraction of electrons to the nucleus is dependent upon these factors:

   i. The nuclear charge (how many protons are present)

   ii. The shielding effect of the inner electrons (the extent to which inner electrons protect the outer electrons from the nuclear charge)

5. Large jumps in successive ionization energies for a single element are observed when passing from one quantum shell to another. In the following example, element X loses 3 electrons relatively easily but the fourth requires much more energy. This is because it is situated in a new quantum shell, closer to the nucleus with less shielding. As a result, we can predict X has three electrons in its outer shell and is therefore in group 13 of the periodic table.

Ionization Energies for Element X (kJ/mol)				
First	Second	Third	Fourth	Fifth
540	1651	2650	14921	17345

6. The following are periodic trends in ionization energy:

    i. When crossing a period from left to right, the ionization energy will steadily increase. This is because the nuclear charge increases (greater positive charge, extra protons) and the electrons are being removed from the same principal quantum level (shell), experiencing no extra shielding, and are therefore held more strongly.

    ii. When ascending a group from bottom to top, the ionization energy will increase because, although there is again an increase in nuclear charge, the outer electrons enter new quantum levels (shells) further away from the nucleus and experience more shielding from the inner electrons and are therefore held less strongly. Shielding is the more important factor. See the following diagram.

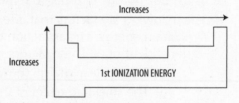

Increases

Increases

1st IONIZATION ENERGY

Metallic character increases to the left and to the bottom of the periodic table, meaning the elements at the bottom of groups 1 and 2 (Cs, Ba, Fr, and Ra) are considered the most metallic. Similarly, the elements in the top right of the periodic table (He, F, and Ne) are the considered the least metallic (most nonmetallic).

IV ELECTRON AFFINITY

A. ELECTRON AFFINITY IS THE QUANTITATIVE MEASUREMENT OF ENERGY CHANGES THAT OCCUR WHEN ADDING ELECTRONS

1. *First electron affinity* is defined as the energy change when 1 mole of gaseous atoms gains 1 mole of electrons to form 1 mole of gaseous ions.

$$X_{(g)} + e^- \rightarrow X^-_{(g)}$$

2. *Second electron affinity* is defined as the energy change accompanying the following process.

$$X^-_{(g)} + e^- \rightarrow X^{2-}_{(g)}$$

3. Electron affinities are measured in units of kJ mol^{-1}. They have both positive (endothermic) and negative (exothermic) values, depending on the species being formed. This indicates that energy may have to be "put in" (positive) or energy may be "released" (negative) when adding electrons.

4. Patterns of electron affinity are less easy to predict than patterns of ionization energy; however, it is useful to know the following:

    i. The overall trend from left to right on the periodic table is an increasing tendency to accept electrons, i.e., that electron affinities become increasingly positive. This makes sense because nonmetals (on the right of the period table) tend to want to form negative ions (by accepting electrons) much more readily than metals (on the left of the table) that generally tend to want to lose electrons and form positive ions. As a result, group 17 (the halogens) have the highest electron affinity values.

    ii. The overall trend within a group is a little more difficult to predict, but as a general rule, values vary little amongst the elements of the same group but with some small increases as one passes from the bottom to the top of a group. See the following diagram.

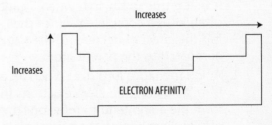

V. ATOMIC AND IONIC SIZE

A. ATOMIC AND IONIC SIZE REFERS TO THE PHYSICAL SIZE OF ATOMS AND IONS

1. As a period is traversed from left to right, the atomic size decreases. This is because the nuclear charge increases (greater positive charge, extra protons) and the subsequent electrons enter the same quantum level, experiencing no extra shielding from inner electrons and are therefore attracted (pulled in) more tightly. See the following diagram.

2. As a group is descended, the atomic size increases. This is because, although there is an increase in the number of protons, there is also an increase in quantum levels, so the electrons are further away from the nucleus and experience more shielding. As a result, the atomic size increases because the greater the number of quantum levels occupied in an atom, the larger the atom.

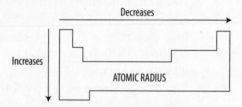

3. Cation (positive ion) size. When an atom loses electrons to form a cation, the remaining electrons will experience less mutual repulsion and as a result they are drawn closer than in the atom and the cation is smaller than the parent atom. It is also true to say that when a cation is formed, an atom often loses a complete valence shell of electrons, which has the effect of decreasing the size of the cationic species compared to the parent atom.

4. Anion (negative ion) size. When an atom gains electrons to form an anion, the extra electrons that have been added to form the anion tend to repel one another. This has the effect of slightly enlarging the new anionic species, making the anion larger than the corresponding atom.

ELECTRONEGATIVITY

A. **ELECTRONEGATIVITY IS A MEASURE OF HOW WELL ATOMS ATTRACT SHARED ELECTRONS**

1. Electronegativity is defined as the ability of an atom within a covalent bond, to attract electrons to itself.

2. Electronegativity increases across a period from left to right and decreases down a group from bottom to top.

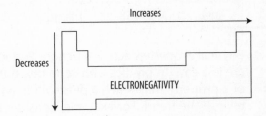

3. Fluorine is the most electronegative element.

4. The noble gases (group 18) are usually omitted from electronegativity discussions because they form so few covalent bonds. See the following diagram.

 PERIODIC PHYSICAL PROPERTIES OF THE ELEMENTS

A. **THERE IS VARIATION IN PHYSICAL PROPERTIES IN GROUPS AND PERIODS**

1. Physical properties within a group. The value of a property tends to change relatively uniformly from top to bottom in a group. For example, consider some of the physical properties of the elements of group 17.

Selected Physical Properties of Group 17 Elements

	Melting Point in Kelvin	Boiling Point in Kelvin	State at Room Temperature	Color
Fluorine	53	85	Gas	Pale green
Chlorine	172	239	Gas	Yellow/green
Bromine	266	332	Liquid	Brown/orange
Iodine	387	458	Solid	Purple/black

2. Physical properties across a period. Periodic physical properties are less easy to predict with certainty, but sometimes the value of a property may reach a peak within a period and then reverse the trend. For example, consider the melting point of the third period elements. Here, the melting points rise to a peak at silicon before falling back to smaller values as at the beginning of the period.

Melting Points of Period 3 Elements

Element	Melting Point in K
Na	371
Mg	922
Al	933
Si	1683
P	863
S	393
Cl	172
Ar	84

MOLECULAR STRUCTURE: LEWIS STRUCTURES, THREE-DIMENSIONAL SHAPES, AND POLARITY

I. DRAWING LEWIS STRUCTURES

A. LEWIS STRUCTURES ARE DIAGRAMS USED TO REPRESENT COVALENTLY BONDED SPECIES THAT SHOW VALENCE ELECTRONS AS DOTS. THE FOLLOWING IS A METHOD FOR CONSTRUCTING THEM:

1. Calculate the total number of valence shell electrons, taking into account any charges present by adding for negative charges, and subtracting for positive charges.

2. In a species with more than two atoms, decide which atom is the central one (this is usually obvious, but if in doubt it will be the least electronegative atom but never hydrogen).

3. Use one pair of electrons (represented by two "dots") to form a covalent bond between each of the terminal (outer) atoms and the central atom.

4. Arrange the remaining electrons to complete the octets of the terminal atoms. (Hydrogen only needs two electrons to complete its valence shell.)

5. Place any remaining electrons on the central atom, if necessary expanding the central atom's octet.

      i. Atoms in period 3 of the periodic table and below, can use empty d orbitals in their valence shell to expand those valence shells beyond just the s and p sub-shells. This is called an *expanded octet*. See the following diagram.

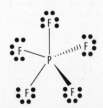

6. If the central atom lacks an octet, form multiple bonds (double or triple) by converting nonbonding electrons from terminal atoms into bonding pairs between the terminal atoms and central atom.

   i. One bonding pair of electrons represents a single covalent bond that in turn can be represented by a single line (–); two bonding pairs represent a double bond represented by a double line (=); and three bonding pairs represent a triple bond represented by a triple line (≡).

7. Some atoms need less than 8 electrons (typically Be and B) and remain *electron deficient* without full octets. An example is BCl_3. See the following diagram.

8. If the covalently bonded species has a charge (usually a polyatomic ion), then use square brackets to enclose the Lewis structure and add the charge as a superscript, as shown in the following diagram.

9. Examples of Lewis structures are shown in the following diagrams.

    i. CO_2

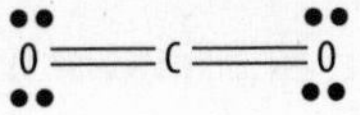

    ii. N_2

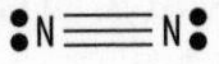

    iii. NH_3

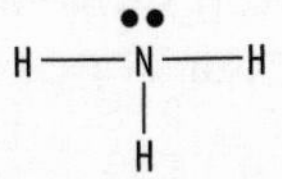

    iv. NH_2OH

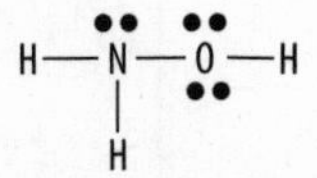

    v. CH_3COOH

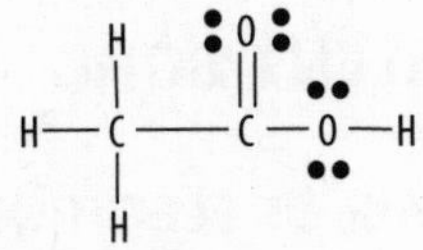

    vi. CH_3OH

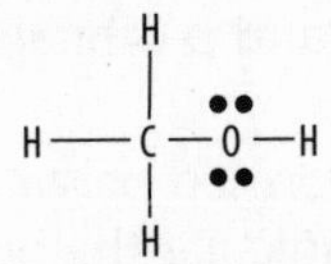

RESONANCE

A. RESONANCE IS USED WHEN MORE THAN ONE FEASIBLE LEWIS STRUCTURE EXISTS

1. Resonance often occurs when a double bond can be positioned in more than one place.
2. Bond lengths and strengths found in the species are "averages" of the single and double bonds present.
3. An example is the carbonate ion, as shown in the following diagram. Bond lengths and strengths are found to be intermediate between single and double bonds and have orders of 1⅓ (i.e., four bonds divided amongst three oxygen atoms).

Resonance Structures of the Carbonate Ion CO_3^{2-}

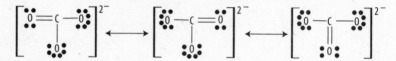

 TYPES OF COVALENT BOND

A. ANY SHARED PAIR OF ELECTRONS IS CONSIDERED TO BE A COVALENT BOND, BUT DIFFERENT TYPES EXIST

1. A sigma (σ) bond is formed between the overlap of two s orbitals or an s and p orbital along the bond axis between two atoms.
2. A pi (π) bond is formed between the overlap of two p orbitals perpendicular the bond axis between two atoms. Pi bonds are weaker than sigma bonds.
3. Single covalent bonds are composed of only sigma bonds, double covalent bonds are composed of one sigma and one pi bond and triple covalent bonds are composed of one sigma and two pi bonds.

SHAPES OF COVALENTLY BONDED SPECIES

A. LEWIS STRUCTURES AND VSEPR ALLOW THE PREDICTION OF THREE-DIMENSIONAL (3D) SHAPES

1. The electron pairs around the central atoms in a covalently bonded species repel one another in order to get as far apart as possible. This is called *valence shell electron pair repulsion,* or *VSEPR.*

2. Determine the 3D shapes of covalently bonded species, as follows:

   i. Draw the Lewis dot structure for the species.

   ii. Count the electron pairs (both bonding and nonbonding) around the central atom.

   iii. Use the following charts to recall the correct shape, name, and bond angles.

Molecular Geometry with Central Atom Having No Lone Electron Pair

Molecular Geometry	Number of lone electron pairs around central atom	Formula	Example	VSEPR Prediction and Bond Angle Measurement
Linear	0	AX_2	CO_2	180° X—A—X
Trigonal Planar	0	AX_3	BF_3	120° X, X, X, A

(continued)

Molecular Geometry with
Central Atom Having No Lone Electron Pair (*continued*)

Molecular Geometry	Number of lone electron pairs around central atom	Formula	Example	VSEPR Prediction and Bond Angle Measurement
Tetrahedral	0	AX_4	CH_4	
Trigonal-bipyramidal	0	AX_5	PF_5	
Octahedral	0	AX_6	SF_6	

Molecular Geometry with Central Atom Having One Lone Electron Pair

Molecular Geometry	Number of lone electron pairs around central atom	Formula	Example	VSEPR Prediction
Bent	1	AX_2E	SeO_2	
Trigonal Pyramidal	1	AX_3E	NH_3	
Seesaw	1	AX_4E	SF_4	
Square-Pyramidal	1	AX_5E	BrF_5	

Molecular Geometry with
Central Atom Having Two Lone Electron Pairs

Molecular Geometry	Number of lone electron pairs around central atom	Formula	Example	VSEPR Prediction
Bent	2	AX_2E_2	H_2O	
T-shape	2	AX_3E_2	ICl_3	
Square Planar	2	AX_4E_2	XeF_4	

Molecular Geometry with
Central Atom Having Three Lone Electron Pairs

Molecular Geometry	Number of lone electron pairs around central atom	Formula	Example	VSEPR Prediction
Linear	3	AX_2E_3	XeF_2	

You must learn and commit to memory the molecular shapes, their names, and bond angles. HOWEVER, if you can use intuition by remembering the principle behind VSEPR, then your life will be easier. For example, ask yourself how do two or three electron pairs around a central atom get as far apart as possible? If it is obvious to you that two electron pairs would spread out to opposite sides of the central atom, and that three electron pairs would arrange themselves in a triangle around the central atom, then you may be able to "work out" the linear and trigonal planar shapes for those species, and the corresponding bond angles of 180° and 120°, without the need for pure memorization.

3. See the following additional notes about Lewis structures, shape, and bond angles:
    i. A nonbonding or lone pair (LP) will repel more strongly than a bonding pair (BP). When comparing bond angles, you can see that this has the effect of altering the bond angles in molecules that have a similar total number of electron pairs, but where the total is comprised of different combinations of bonding and lone pairs.
        a) For example, CH_4 (4BP, 0LP), NH_3 (3BP, 1LP), and H_2O (2BP, 2LP) all have a total of four pairs around the central atom, but have bond angles of approximately 109.5°, 107.5° and 104.5°, respectively.
    ii. For the purposes of predicting shape, multiple bonds can be considered as single bonds.
        a) For example, carbon dioxide can be considered to be surrounded by two electron pairs (negative centers) and is therefore linear.
4. Hybridization:
    i. Atomic orbitals are mixed to form hybrid orbitals that aid symmetry.
    ii. Hybridization can be determined by considering the total number of electron pairs around the central atom, and then using the appropriate number of s, p, and d orbitals.
    iii. When considering hybridization, count double and triple bonds as single bonds because pi bonds are caused by overlap of unhybridized p orbitals.

iv. A total of two pairs = sp hybrid; three = sp²
    hybrid; four = sp³ hybrid; five = sp³d hybrid; and
    six = sp³d² hybrid.

V. POLAR BONDS AND POLAR MOLECULES

A. WHEN SEPARATE ENDS OF A BOND OR MOLECULE CARRY A PARTIAL POSITIVE OR NEGATIVE CHARGE, IT IS SAID TO BE *POLAR*

1. Dipoles are created within covalent bonds by a difference in electronegativity.
    i. More electronegative atoms attract the shared pair of electrons toward themselves, and as a result that end of the bond becomes slightly negative.
    ii. The movement of electrons away from the more electropositive elements leaves them relatively positive.
    iii. Bonds where the atoms at either end have the same or very small differences in electronegativity (around a difference of 0.4 or less), are considered *nonpolar*.
2. In order for a molecule to be polar overall, polar bonds must be present, PLUS the dipoles should NOT cancel out due to symmetry.
3. The dipole moment can be indicated by an arrow that points toward the negative charge center with the tail of the arrow indicating the positive charge center, or by using δ+ and δ− to indicate small areas of positive and negative charge, as shown in the following diagram.

4. For example, consider water. Opposite ends of the molecules carry different charges and there is no canceling of the dipoles, so the molecule is polar as shown in the following diagram.

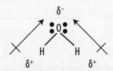

5. Now consider hexane and carbon tetrachloride, neither of which are polar molecules but this is due to different reasons.

    i. In hexane (C_6H_{14}), carbon and hydrogen have very similar electronegativities and as a result the bonds are effectively nonpolar.

    ii. In carbon tetrachloride (CCl_4), on the other hand, has four polar C–Cl bonds but because of its symmetrical shape is nonpolar overall. The partial positive charge is located at the center of the molecule and the partial negative charges equally spread around it, causing the dipoles to cancel.

Test Tip

A molecule that has a single lone pair will always be polar, since there will be nothing similar to cancel out the large area of negative charge that the lone pair introduces.

BONDING: IONIC, COVALENT, AND METALLIC BONDS

I. IONIC BONDING

A. IONIC BONDS ARE STRONG *INTRA*BONDS FORMED BETWEEN METALS AND NONMETALS

1. Atoms have equal numbers of protons and electrons and consequently have no overall charge.

2. When atoms lose or gain electrons, (in order to achieve full s and p sub-shells or a "noble gas structure" and stability), the proton/electron numbers are unbalanced, causing the particles to become charged. These charged particles are called *ions*.

3. The strong electrostatic forces between the charged particles are called *ionic bonds*.

4. Because the electrostatic forces are large, the ionic bond is a strong one.

5. Metal atoms have a tendency to lose electrons to form positive ions and nonmetal atoms have a tendency gain electrons to form negative ions; therefore, the ionic bond is usually formed between metals and nonmetals.

6. Ionic substances form regular, cubic arrangements called *giant ionic lattices,* as shown in the following diagram.

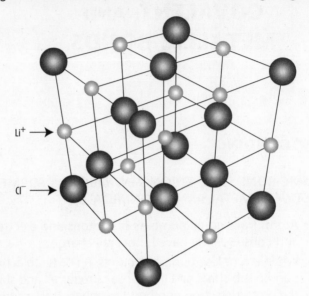

Li⁺ →

Cl⁻ →

7. The *lattice energy* is a quantitative measure of the attraction between ions in an ionic lattice.

II. COVALENT BONDING

A. COVALENT BONDS ARE STRONG *INTRA*BONDS FORMED BETWEEN TWO NONMETALS

1. Covalent bonding involves the sharing of electrons between atoms to form discrete molecules.

2. In covalent bonding, atoms once again want to achieve full s and p sub-shells, this time by joining together and sharing valence electrons. Full s and p sub-shells are called *octets.*

3. One shared pair of electrons represents a single covalent bond; two shared pairs represent a double bond; and three shared pairs represent a triple bond.
4. Covalent bonds usually occur between atoms that are nonmetals.
5. Any electron pairs that occur in the valence shell of an atom but do not form a bond with another atom are called *nonbonding electrons* or *lone pairs*.
6. The structures of molecules that contain covalent bonds are described by the use of Lewis diagrams where "dots" are used to represent valence electrons, as shown in the following diagram. Also, see Chapter 6.

Group 1 ns^1	Group 2 ns^2	Group 13 ns^{2}np^1	Group 14 ns^{2}np^2	Group 15 ns^{2}np^3	Group 16 ns^{2}np^4	Group 17 ns^{2}np^5	Group 18 ns^{2}np^6
Li •	• Be •	• B̊ •	• C̈ •	• N̈ •	̈Ö•	̈Cl̈•	̈N̈ë

Ionic and covalent bonds are both strong bonds that can be described as intrabonds, *i.e., bonds that exist* within *a compound. However, covalently bonded, molecular substances (i.e., those that do not form giant networks) have low melting and boiling points because they are only attracted to one another with weak inter-molecular forces. For example, when water boils, only relatively weak intermolecular forces are being broken, NOT the very strong covalent bonds between hydrogen and oxygen atoms within the molecule. It is very important to understand the distinctions between* intrabond breaking *and* interbond breaking. *Many questions will expect you to make this distinction.*

III. **METALLIC BONDING**

A. METALLIC BONDING REFERS TO THE BONDING AND STRUCTURE PRESENT IN METALS

1. A metal's structure can be considered to be a close-packed lattice of positive ions surrounded by a "sea" of moving electrons, as shown in the following diagram.

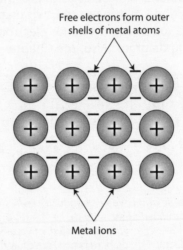

Free electrons form outer shells of metal atoms

Metal ions

2. These electrons and their movement cause metals to be good conductors of electricity.
3. The close-packed ions make them good conductors of heat.
4. The metallic bond is the electrostatic attraction between the positive and negative charges.
5. The flexibility of these bonds makes metals malleable and ductile.

> *Look out for questions that ask about the properties of metals related to their bonding and structure. Good conduction of heat and electricity, malleability and ductility, along with luster (shininess) are all typical properties of metals. Recognizing these traits in test questions will help you raise your score.*

RELATIONSHIPS BETWEEN THE **BONDING** AND STRUCTURE OF **SOLIDS** AND **THEIR PROPERTIES**

I. **SOLID STRUCTURES AND PROPERTIES**—Variations in bond type lead to different structures in solids.

A. **GIANT ATOMIC STRUCTURES**—These are structures where atoms are bonded to one another with covalent bonds in a massive (or giant), continuous network. Examples include diamond and graphite.

1. Diamond is based upon a tetrahedral unit where all of the carbon atoms are bonded to four others with very strong covalent bonds in a huge macrostructure.
    i. Large numbers of strong covalent bonds makes diamond very strong and hard and gives it a high melting and boiling point.
2. Graphite has a layered structure where each carbon atom is covalently bonded to three others in each plane. The structure leads to specific properties:
    i. It will conduct electricity only in one plane. In the graphite structure, each carbon is only bonded to three others. This leaves one of each carbon atoms' valence electrons "free." These electrons are spread out over each layer (delocalized). This leads to a "sea" of electrons similar to that in the metallic structure and is responsible for graphite's ability to conduct electricity along the layers. Because the electrons cannot move between layers, there is no conduction from one layer to another.
    ii. It can be used as a lubricant. Weak London dispersion forces (see Chapter 9) hold the layers in graphite together. As a result, they can slide over one another, making graphite a good lubricant.

B. IONIC STRUCTURES—These are structures where a giant lattice of ions is held together by strong electrostatic interactions (ionic bonds) between the opposite charges. An example is sodium chloride.

1. The strong ionic bonds give ionic solids high melting and boiling points.

2. They can only conduct electricity when molten or in solution because when they are in the solid state, the ions are rigidly held and cannot move. When molten or in solution, the ions are free to move so electricity can be conducted.

3. The charged particles present in an ionic solid explain how and why ionic solids dissolve in water. When an ionic solid dissolves, the polar water molecules penetrate the lattice and attach themselves to the ions. The process is called *hydration* and the ions are said to be *hydrated*.

You may have heard the phrase "like dissolves like"; this refers to the fact that charged substances (like ionic solids) tend to dissolve in polar (charged) solvents. Remember the phrase—it's a good rule of thumb.

C. MOLECULAR STRUCTURES—These are structures where molecules are attracted to one another with weak intermolecular forces. An example is iodine.

1. Weak intermolecular forces hold the molecules in place in the solid.

2. Weak forces mean that molecular solids tend to have very low melting points because there is only a weak interaction between its molecules, and they tend to be soft.

3. No charged particles are present, making molecular solids nonconductors.

Most test questions expect you to be able to relate observed physical properties such as melting and boiling points, electrical conductivity, hardness, and water solubility to the type of structure and bonding present. Focus your review on the relationships between structure and properties.

INTERMOLECULAR FORCES: HYDROGEN BONDING, DIPOLE– DIPOLE FORCES, AND LONDON DISPERSION FORCES

I. **INTERMOLECULAR FORCES (IMFs)**—These are weak forces between molecules that rely on small electrostatic interactions.

A. **HYDROGEN BONDING**—Hydrogen atoms, when bonded to certain elements create unusually large intermolecular attractions.

1. Hydrogen is an exceptional element in that when it forms a covalent bond, its electron is held to one side of the nucleus leaving the other side completely exposed.

2. Any approaching negatively charged group can get very close to the hydrogen nucleus and this produces an unexpectedly large electrostatic attraction.

3. These electrostatic attractions are exaggerated when H is bonded to a more electronegative element that is small enough to allow a significant intermolecular interaction, i.e., fluorine, oxygen, or nitrogen. Such exaggerated, intermolecular, electrostatic attractions are called *hydrogen bonds*.

4. The occurrence of hydrogen bonds has the following two important consequences, both of which are explained by the increased attraction between molecules caused by hydrogen bonding, making it more difficult to separate them.

      i. It gives substances that contain them anomalously high boiling points, as shown in the following table.

Hydrogen Halide	Normal Boiling Pt, °C
HF*	19
HCl	−85
HBr	−67
HI	−35

*High BP attributed to hydrogen bonding

   ii. Substances that contain them tend to have increased viscosity.

As soon as you see a hydrogen atom directly connected to N, O, or F, think "hydrogen bonding," BUT be careful! Just because a chemical formula has hydrogen and one of those elements present, it does not necessarily mean that hydrogen is connected DIRECTLY to N, O, or F. Check to see which atoms are connected to one another. For example, H_3COCH_3 does not have hydrogen bonding (hydrogen atoms bonded to carbon atoms), but CH_3CH_2OH, does (hydrogen atoms bonded to oxygen atoms).

   5. Hydrogen bonds are the strongest of the (weak) intermolecular forces.

B. DIPOLE–DIPOLE FORCES—Permanent dipoles in adjacent molecules attract one another.

   1. Molecules with polar bonds (caused by differences in electronegativity) and dipoles that do not cancel will have permanent dipoles.

   2. When molecules that have permanent dipoles approach one another, they will arrange themselves so that the negative and the positive ends of the molecules attract one another.

   3. The attractions are called *dipole–dipole forces*.

   4. Dipole–dipole interactions are intermediate in strength in terms of the (weak) intermolecular forces.

C. **LONDON DISPERSION FORCES (LDFs)**—These are very small electrostatic interactions between molecules when no permanent dipoles are present.

1. London dispersion forces are small electrostatic forces that are caused by movement of electrons within the covalent bonds of molecules that would otherwise have no permanent dipole.

2. As one molecule approaches another, the electrons of one or both are temporarily displaced owing to their mutual repulsion. This movement causes small, temporary dipoles to be set up that attract one another. These attractions are called *London dispersion forces.*

3. These dispersion forces increase with the number of electrons in the molecule. This leads to more dispersion forces, greater attraction and therefore higher melting and boiling points among molecules with larger numbers of electrons when compared to molecules with smaller numbers of electrons.

4. London dispersion forces are the weakest of the (weak) intermolecular forces.

Recall that ALL substances will have some degree of London dispersion force, but text questions usually focus on recognition of a single IMF. You should immediately recognize hydrogen bonding whenever H is directly connected to N, O, or F and dipole–dipole interactions when there are significant differences in electronegativity and the dipoles do not cancel. Molecules with very small or no differences in electronegativity will only exhibit LDFs as their IMFs.

PART III:
STATES OF MATTER

GASES: THE KINETIC MOLECULAR THEORY

I. KINETIC MOLECULAR THEORY

A. THE KINETIC MOLECULAR THEORY IS USED AS A BASIS FOR EXPLAINING THE OBSERVED PROPERTIES OF GASES. IT STATES THE FOLLOWING:

1. Gases are composed of tiny particles (atoms or molecules) whose size is negligible compared to the average distance between them. This means the following:

    i. The volume of the individual gas particles themselves can be assumed to be negligible compared to the volume of the container.

    ii. The total volume that the gas fills is almost all empty space. The fact that gases are compressible is consistent with this part of the kinetic molecular theory.

2. Gas particles move randomly, in straight lines, in all directions, and at various speeds.

3. The forces of attraction or repulsion between two gas particles are extremely weak or negligible, except when they collide.

4. When particles collide with one another, the collisions are elastic (i.e., no kinetic energy is lost).

    i. Elastic collisions are consistent with the observation that gases, when left alone in a container, do not spontaneously convert into a liquid.

5. The collisions of the gas particles with the walls of the container create the gas pressure.
   - i. Pressure = force per unit area.
   - ii. Common units of pressure are:
     - a) Atmospheres (atm)
     - b) Millimeters of mercury (mmHg)
     - c) Torr (torr)
     - d) **Note:** 1.00 atm = 760 mmHg = 760 torr.
6. The average kinetic energy of a gas particle is proportional to the Kelvin temperature.
   - i. Perform all calculations involving gases with temperatures converted to Kelvin, thus eliminating the problem of negative volumes, negative pressures, and negative moles.
   - ii. K = °C + 273.15

It is VITALLY important to remember to always use Kelvin as the unit of temperature in all gas calculations. Make a note of it! Also, make a careful note of the units of pressure given in a question. Although (unlike temperature) they can be variable, it is important to use the correct units in the correct situation.

II. IDEAL GASES AND REAL GASES

A. THERE ARE LIMITATIONS TO ASSUMPTIONS THAT GAS PARTICLES DO NOT ATTRACT ONE ANOTHER AND DO NOT TAKE UP SIGNIFICANT VOLUME WHEN COMPARED TO THE WHOLE

1. Gases that *do* behave according to those assumptions are called *ideal gases*.
2. Generally, gases behave "ideally" under the following conditions:
   - i. High temperatures
   - ii. Low pressures

3. Gases that start to show deviations from ideal behavior are called *real gases*. At low temperatures and high pressures, many gases act as real gases and have the following characteristics:

   i. Particles that *do* take up significant volume when compared to the volume of the container
   ii. Particles that *do* have attractive forces between them

4. This means that real gases begin to behave in a manner that shows some inconsistencies when compared to the assumptions kinetic molecular theory makes about ideal gases.

Test Tip

It is unlikely that you will encounter many questions about real gases on the test, so focus your studying on the characteristics of ideal gases.

GASES: GAS LAW RELATIONSHIPS

I. PRESSURE AND VOLUME RELATIONSHIPS: BOYLE'S LAW

A. BOYLE'S LAW STATES THAT AT CONSTANT TEMPERATURE AND WITH A CONSTANT MASS OF GAS, PRESSURE IS INVERSELY PROPORTIONAL TO VOLUME

1. $PV = $ a constant
2. If the pressure and volume of a gas are known initially, and one of the variables is changed, then the new conditions can be calculated by using $P_1 V_1 = P_2 V_2$. See the following diagram. *(P_1 and V_1 are the original conditions and P_2 and V_2 are the new conditions. Units of pressure and volume must be the same on each side of the equation.)*

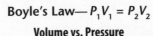

Boyle's Law—$P_1V_1 = P_2V_2$

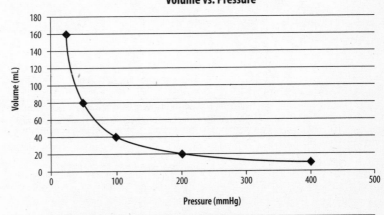

Volume vs. Pressure

Note in the graph above that when the pressure is doubled, the volume is halved. Therefore, the mathematics of solving a Boyle's Law problem is easy.

II. VOLUME AND TEMPERATURE RELATIONSHIPS: CHARLES'S LAW

A. CHARLES'S LAW STATES THAT AT CONSTANT PRESSURE AND WITH A CONSTANT MASS OF GAS, VOLUME IS DIRECTLY PROPORTIONAL TO TEMPERATURE

1. $\dfrac{V}{T}$ = a constant

2. If the volume and temperature of a gas are known initially, and one of the variables is changed, the new conditions can be calculated by using $\dfrac{V_1}{T_1} = \dfrac{V_2}{T_2}$. See the following diagram.

(V$_1$ and T$_1$ are the original conditions and V$_2$ and T$_2$ are the new conditions. Units of volume must be the same on each side of the equation and temperature must be in Kelvin.)

Charles's Law— $\dfrac{V_1}{T_1} = \dfrac{V_2}{T_2}$

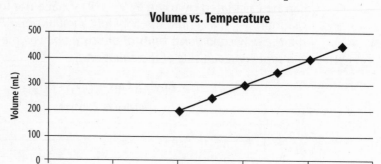

Volume vs. Temperature

Note in the graph above that when the temperature is doubled, the volume is doubled. Therefore, the mathematics of solving a Charles's Law problem is easy.

VOLUME AND MOLES RELATIONSHIPS: AVOGADRO'S LAW

A. AVOGADRO'S LAW STATES THAT AT CONSTANT TEMPERATURE AND CONSTANT PRESSURE, VOLUME IS DIRECTLY PROPORTIONAL TO THE NUMBER OF MOLES OF GAS PRESENT

1. $\dfrac{V}{n}$ = a constant

2. If the volume and number of moles of a gas are known initially, and one of the variables is changed, the new conditions can be calculated by using $\dfrac{V_1}{n_1} = \dfrac{V_2}{n_2}$. See the following diagram. *(V$_1$ and n$_1$ are the original conditions and V$_2$ and n$_2$ are the new conditions. Units of volume and moles must be the same on each side of the equation.)*

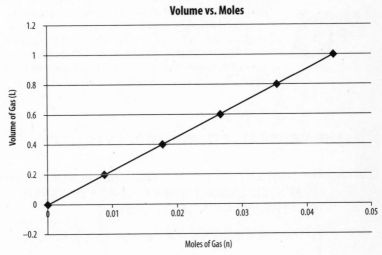

Avogadro's Law— $\dfrac{V_1}{n_1} = \dfrac{V_2}{n_2}$

Volume vs. Moles

IV. PRESSURE AND TEMPERATURE RELATIONSHIPS: GAY-LUSSAC'S LAW

A. GAY-LUSSAC'S LAW STATES THAT, AT CONSTANT VOLUME AND WITH A CONSTANT MASS OF GAS, PRESSURE IS DIRECTLY PROPORTIONAL TO TEMPERATURE

1. $\dfrac{P}{T} = $ a constant

2. If the pressure and temperature of a gas are known initially, and one of the variables is changed, the new conditions can be calculated by using $\dfrac{P_1}{T_1} = \dfrac{P_2}{T_2}$. *(P$_1$ and T$_1$ are the original conditions and P$_2$ and T$_2$ are the new conditions. Units of pressure must be the same on each side of the equation and temperature must be in Kelvin.)*

A very useful strategy in dealing with gas calculations is to make a list of the values that are given in any question, plus noting the variable that is unknown. Very often, this will help you to decide which equation to use. For example, if values for an initial pressure, new pressure, and initial volume are given in the question (i.e., P$_1$, P$_2$, and V$_1$), and the question is asking for the new (final) volume (i.e., V$_2$ is the unknown), then it should become obvious that Boyle's law should be used (i.e., apply P$_1$ V$_1$ = P$_2$ V$_2$). Make a list—it often helps!

V. THE GENERAL/COMBINED GAS EQUATION

A. IN ADDITION TO THE INDIVIDUAL RELATIONSHIPS PRESENTED EARLIER, THEY CAN BE COMBINED TOGETHER IN A SINGLE EQUATION:

1. The general/combined gas equation is as follows:

$$\frac{P_1 V_1}{n_1 T_1} = \frac{P_2 V_2}{n_2 T_2}$$

2. If the number of moles of gas in an experiment is constant (frequently the case), then $n_1 = n_2$ and therefore n_1 and

n_2 can be left out of the equation. When this happens, the equation becomes the following:

$$\frac{P_1 V_1}{T_1} = \frac{P_2 V_2}{T_2}$$

(In these equations, P_1, V_1, T_1, and n_1 are the original conditions and P_2, V_2, T_2, and n_2 are the new conditions. Units must be the same on each side of the equation and temperature must be in Kelvin.)

VI. GRAHAM'S LAW OF EFFUSION AND DIFFUSION

A. EFFUSION AND DIFFUSION ARE BEHAVIORS OF GASES THAT ARE VERY SIMILAR IN THEIR ACTIONS AND THEIR MATHEMATICAL RELATIONSHIPS

1. Effusion is the process in which a gas escapes from a vessel by passing through a very small opening.

2. Graham's law of effusion states that the rate of effusion is inversely proportional to the square roots of their respective densities and molecular masses, as shown in the following equations.

$$\frac{\text{Rate of effusion of A}}{\text{Rate of effusion of B}} = \sqrt{\frac{\text{density of B}}{\text{density of A}}} = \sqrt{\frac{\text{Molar mass of B}}{\text{Molar mass of A}}}$$

3. Diffusion is the process by which a homogeneous mixture is formed by the random mixing of two different gases.

4. Graham's law of diffusion states that the rate of diffusion is inversely proportional to the square roots of their respective densities and molecular masses, as shown in the following equations.

$$\frac{\text{Rate 1}}{\text{Rate 2}} = \sqrt{\frac{\text{density of 2}}{\text{density of 1}}} = \sqrt{\frac{\text{Molar mass}}{\text{s of 2}}}$$

Take care and note the relative positions of A and B and 1 and 2 on each side of the preceding equations.

MOLAR VOLUME, DENSITY, AND **STOICHIOMETRY** OF **GASES**

I. **THE IDEAL GAS LAW**

A. MOST GASES OBEY THIS LAW AT TEMPERATURES ABOVE 273.15 K AND AT PRESSURES OF 1.00 ATM OR LOWER

1. $PV = nRT$ (where R is the universal gas constant)

2. This equation is used when conditions are fixed and not changing. (See Chapter 11 Gases: Gas Law Relationships for equations that can be used under changing conditions)

3. This equation is useful because it can be manipulated to include other variables.

    i. n (number of moles) can be replaced by $\dfrac{mass}{molar\ mass}$ to give:

$$PV = \frac{mass}{molar\ mass}\ RT$$

This is useful in calculations involving the molar mass of a gas.

    ii. Because density $= \dfrac{mass}{volume}$,

    then density $= \dfrac{(P)(molar\ mass)}{RT}$.

Test Tip

When using the ideal gas equation, the units of R should be carefully noted. The most usual value given for R is 0.0821 atm L mol⁻¹ K⁻¹. This is important because it means that in order for units to cancel properly in the equation, whenever one uses R = 0.0821 atm L mol⁻¹ K⁻¹, then pressure must be in units of atmospheres, volume must be in units of liters, and (as ALWAYS), temperature must in units of Kelvin. (It is also true that moles must be in units of mol, but it would be a very odd question that would not give moles in these units to begin with.)

II. DALTON'S LAW OF PARTIAL PRESSURES

A. DALTON'S LAW STATES THAT IN A MIXTURE OF GASES, THE TOTAL PRESSURE EXERTED BY THE MIXTURE IS EQUAL TO THE SUM OF THE INDIVIDUAL PARTIAL PRESSURES OF EACH GAS

1. $P_{total} = P_1 + P_2 + P_3$ and so on.
2. Assuming ideal behavior and using the ideal gas equation, the relationship can be simplified to:

$$P_{total} = n_{total} \frac{RT}{V}$$

3. An alternative treatment is to apply $PV = nRT$ to each gas individually, and then add the individual pressures together.
4. Dalton's law is especially important to use when collecting a gas over water, as shown in the following diagram. When a gas is collected over water, the pressure in the collection vessel will have TWO components: the pressure of the gas collected, PLUS the pressure of the relatively small amount of water vapor present. Using Dalton's law of partial pressures, the total pressure in the vessel = pressure of the collected gas + water vapor pressure. Because we are usually interested in the pressure of the collected gas, it is necessary to subtract the water vapor pressure from the total pressure in order to calculate the pressure of the collected gas.

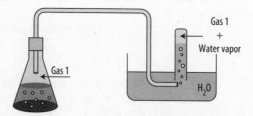

III. MOLAR VOLUME

A. UNDER STANDARD CONDITIONS OF TEMPERATURE
   AND PRESSURE (STP), APPLYING THE DATA PRESSURE
   (P) = 1.00 ATM, TEMPERATURE (T) = 273.15 K, THE GAS
   CONSTANT (R) = 0.0821 L ATM K^{-1} MOL^{-1}, AND NUMBER
   OF MOLES (n) = 1.00 MOL TO THE IDEAL GAS EQUATION,
   YOU CAN FIND THE MOLAR VOLUME (V)

   1. A simple calculation finds the value of molar volume at STP
      to be = 22.4 L.
   2. That is to say, 1 mole of any ideal gas at STP will occupy
      a volume of 22.4 L.

Test Tip

> Be SURE standard conditions of temperature (273.15 K) and
> pressure (1.00 atm) are in play when applying the relationship
> of 1.00 mol occupies 22.4 L.

IV. GAS STOICHIOMETRY

A. HERE, WE APPLY THE STP RELATIONSHIP OF 1.00 MOL
   OF ANY GAS OCCUPIES 22.4 L TO GAS STOICHIOMETRY

   1. As long as STP prevails, then apply the conversion factor

      of $\dfrac{1\,\text{mol of gas}}{22.4\,\text{L}}$ or $\dfrac{22.4\,\text{L}}{1\,\text{mol of gas}}$ to convert between units.

   2. These relationships allow the direct conversion of volume to
      moles and moles to volume.

PHASE CHANGES
AND PHASE DIAGRAMS

I. PHASE CHANGES

A. PHASE CHANGES AND ENERGY

1. A phase (or state of matter) can be converted to another phase by applying a change in temperature and/or pressure. Each transition between the phases has a name. Note that the energy changes in iv, v, and vi will be equal and opposite to those in i, ii, and iii, respectively.

   i. Solid to liquid, or *melting*. The amount of energy required to convert 1 mole of a solid to a liquid is known as the *molar enthalpy of fusion*, ΔH_{fusion}.

   ii. Liquid to gas, or *vaporization*. The amount of energy required to convert 1 mole of a liquid to a gas is known as the *molar enthalpy of vaporization*, $\Delta H_{vaporization}$.

   iii. Solid to gas (directly, with no liquid phase), or *sublimation*. The amount of energy required to convert 1 mole of a solid to a gas is known as the *molar enthalpy of sublimation*, $\Delta H_{sublimation}$.

   iv. Liquid to solid, or *freezing*

   v. Gas to liquid, or *condensing*

   vi. Gas to solid (directly, with no liquid phase), or *reverse sublimation, resublimation,* or *deposition*

Test Tip

Fusion is no more than a fancy word for melting, and although they are slightly different things, vaporization is often used interchangeably with boiling. (Vaporization is actually the process of gas formation from liquid OR solid, and as such is technically really only the same as boiling IF the vaporization takes place AT the boiling point.)

2. The Nature of the Particles in Each Phase

    i. Solids have fixed volumes, fixed shapes, and are incompressible. Their particles do not have much energy, do not move much, and do not diffuse to any extent.

    ii. Gases have no fixed volume or fixed shape and take on the volume and shape of their container. They are highly compressible. Their particles have relatively large energies, move a great deal, and will diffuse readily.

    iii. Liquids have a definite volume but take the shape of their container. Liquids represent an intermediate state between solids and gases in terms of their particles' energy, movement, and ability to diffuse. They are virtually incompressible.

3. Conditions of temperature and pressure, and how they relate to a particular phase are summarized in phase diagrams.

II. PHASE DIAGRAMS

A. GENERAL PRINCIPLES

1. Three areas are defined on a phase diagram that represent each of the three phases.

2. A line represents the conditions of temperature and pressure under which two phases can exist together in equilibrium.

3. Any point on the solid–liquid line represents the melting/freezing point at that particular pressure.

4. Any point on the liquid–gas line represents the boiling/condensing point at that particular pressure.

5. The *triple point* describes the conditions of temperature and pressure under which all three phases can coexist.

6. The *critical point* describes the maximum temperature that a liquid of the substance can exist. Above this temperature,

the difference between the liquid and the gas largely disappears, and the substance is called a *supercritical fluid*.

B. COMMON PHASE DIAGRAMS

1. See the following phase diagram for H_2O.

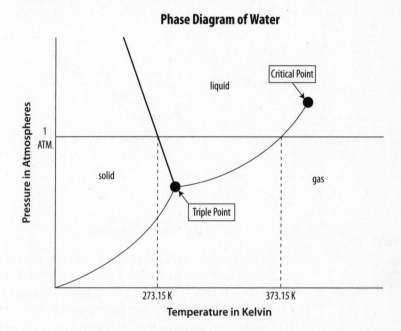

Phase Diagram of Water

i. Continuously heating solid H_2O at 1 atm (normal pressure) causes a phase change from solid to liquid to gas; i.e., the substance DOES pass through the liquid phase between solid and gas phases (compare this to solid CO_2).

ii. The line separating the solid and liquid phases has a negative slope, which indicates that the solid is less dense than the liquid; i.e., that solid H_2O (ice) floats in liquid H_2O (water).

2. See the following phase diagram for CO_2.

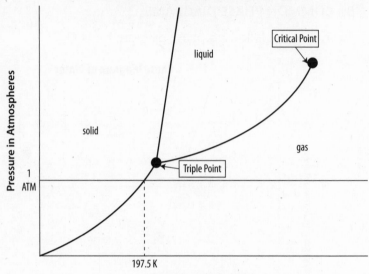

Phase Diagram of Carbon Dioxide

i. Continuously heating solid carbon dioxide at 1 atm (normal pressure) causes a phase change from solid to gas WITHOUT passing through the liquid phase. This is called *sublimation* (compare to solid H_2O).

ii. The line separating the solid and liquid phases has a positive slope which, indicates that the solid is more dense than the liquid; i.e., solid CO_2 would sink in liquid CO_2.

The phase diagrams for water and carbon dioxide are the classic examples that are commonly used in tests; you should become familiar with them. The usual comparisons that are made are the following:

1. *That a pressure of 1 atm is above the triple point for water, so sublimation does not occur but is below the triple point for carbon dioxide and sublimation does occur*

2. *That the solid–liquid lines have different slopes: negative for water, which makes solid H_2O less dense than liquid H_2O; but positive for carbon dioxide, which makes solid CO_2 more dense than liquid CO_2*

SOLUTIONS: MOLARITY AND **PERCENT** BY **MASS** CONCENTRATIONS

I. MOLARITY

A. MOLARITY IS ONE METHOD OF QUANTITATIVELY ASSESSING A SOLUTION

1. A solution is made when a solute (the substance dissolving), usually a solid or a sometimes a liquid, dissolves in a solvent (the medium in which the substance is dissolved), which is usually water.

2. The concentration of a solution can be measured in terms of the number of grams of the solute that has been dissolved in a particular volume of the solution, or more often, in terms of the number of moles of the solute in a particular volume of the solution. Typical units for these concentrations are g/L (g L^{-1}) or mol/L (mol L^{-1}), respectively.

3. The method of expressing the concentration of a solution in mol L^{-1} is the most common and is called *molarity*.

4. Molarity is given the symbol, M.

5. Units of M are expressed as being *molar*, so, for example, a solution that has a concentration of 0.250 mol L^{-1} can be called a *0.250 molar solution*.

6. When concentration is measured in mol L^{-1} (or M), and volume is measured in L, then, for solutions, the moles of solute can be calculated by applying:

$$\text{moles} = (\text{concentration}) \times (\text{volume})$$

It is very common for the concentrations of solutions to be expressed in units of M, and for volumes of those solutions to be expressed in units of mL. When this is the case, be sure to convert mL to L before multiplying by the molarity in order to correctly calculate the moles.

II. PERCENT BY MASS

A. PERCENT BY MASS IS ANOTHER METHOD OF QUANTITATIVELY ASSESSING A SOLUTION

1. A solution is comprised of a solute and a solvent component.
2. As a result, the total mass of a solution is comprised of the mass of the solute plus the mass of the solvent.
3. Expressing the mass of the solute as a percentage of the total mass of the solution is called the *percent by mass*. See the following example.

$$\% \text{ by mass} = \frac{\text{mass of solute}}{\text{total mass of solution}} \times 100$$

4. Here is an example calculation. What is the percent by mass of NaCl of a solution in which 2.00 g of sodium chloride, NaCl, is dissolved in 100. mL of water? The density of water should be taken as 1.00 g/mL.

    i. Mass of solvent (water) = (100. mL) × (1.00 g/mL) = 100 g.

    ii. Total mass of solution = mass of solvent (water) + mass of solute (NaCl) = 100. g + 2.00 g = 102 g.

    iii. $\% \text{ by mass of NaCl} = \dfrac{2.00 \text{ g}}{102. \text{ g}} \times 100 = 1.96\%.$

Test Tip

Percent by mass should result in an answer that is less than 100%. This is a good lesson in checking your answer to any calculation to see if it makes sense. It's a good habit to get into.

SOLUTION PREPARATION AND SOLUTION STOICHIOMETRY

I. DILUTION AND SOLUTION STOICHIOMETRY

A. PREPARING A SOLUTION

1. Often, a solution is prepared by adding water to another, more concentrated, solution. The process is called *dilution*.

2. For example, if 4.0 L of a 2.0 M solution was required, it could be prepared by adding water to (diluting) a 10. M (more concentrated) solution.

3. Calculations involving dilution can be broken down into three steps.

   i. Calculate the number of moles present in the final, diluted solution, by applying:

   $$moles = (concentration) \times (volume).$$

   ii. Because the moles calculated in (i) must have all originated in the more concentrated solution, use the value calculated in (i) to calculate the required volume of the more concentrated solution by reapplying the following formula:

   $$moles = (concentration) \times (volume)$$

   But this time, apply it to the original, more concentrated solution.

   iii. A question could ask for the volume of water that must be added to the concentrated solution. This is simply the difference between the volume of the final, diluted solution and the volume of the concentrated solution that was used to make the final solution.

3. Following is an example of a dilution calculation.

    i. Question: Calculate the volume of water that must be added to prepare 2.0 L of 3.0 M KOH from an original, concentrated solution that has a molarity of 8.0 M.

        a) The final solution must contain (3.0 M) × (2.0 L) = 6.0 mols of KOH.

        b) Because all of those moles of KOH originated in the concentrated solution, reapplying moles = (concentration) × (volume), the volume (in L) of the original concentrated solution that contains 6.0 mols of KOH = $\dfrac{6.0 \text{ mols}}{8.0 \text{ mol/L}}$ = 0.75 L.

        c) So, by taking 0.75 L of the original, concentrated solution and adding 1.25 L of water to make the solution up to 2.00 L, the final, diluted solution will have a concentration (molarity) = $\dfrac{6.0 \text{ mol}}{2.0 \text{ L}}$ = 3.0 M.

B. GLASSWARE USED IN SOLUTION PREPARATION

1. Very precise measurements are required in when making solutions, and as a result you must use glassware that is accurately graduated.

2. A volumetric flask is the vessel in which the solute and solvent are mixed in order to prepare the solution. It is accurately graduated to produce a solution with a very precise total volume. See the following diagram.

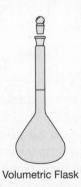

Volumetric Flask

3. A volumetric pipette is used for transferring accurately measured quantities of solutions from one vessel to another. It is used in conjunction with a pipette filler. See the following diagram.

Volumetric Pipette

4. A burette is used for delivering precise amounts of solution, usually in a titration.

Burette

Questions sometimes try to catch you out by asking about glassware and precise measurements. Remember that beakers and graduated cylinders do not offer precise measurements when compared to pipettes and burets, and that any procedure that requires precision should involve the use of the three pieces of apparatus listed above.

II. DILUTION AND SAFETY

A. DILUTING ACIDS

1. When diluting a concentrated acid, it is often found that combining water and the acid is a very exothermic process, i.e., one that releases lots of energy.

2. In some cases, the energy produced can be very significant and may even cause the water present to turn into the gaseous state (steam). As the steam leaves the system, it can cause a "spray" of concentrated acid and as such can represent a significant safety hazard.

3. In order to minimize this hazard, it is important to always add acid TO water, and NOT water to acid.

There is a common saying to help you remember the way to dilute acids: **"Do as you ought to ('oughta'), add acid to water."**

4. The dilution sequence of adding a relative small amount of (hazardous) acid to a relatively large volume of (nonhazardous) water ensures that the heat generated is kept to a minimum, and that acid remains in the presence of as much water as possible until it reaches the desired concentration. This will minimize the risk of accidents.

FACTORS AFFECTING SOLUBILITY OF SOLIDS, LIQUIDS, AND GASES

SOLUBILITY OF SOLIDS AND LIQUIDS

A. TEMPERATURE AND PRESSURE CONSIDERATIONS

1. In general, solids and liquids become increasingly soluble with increased temperature of solvent. See the following diagram.

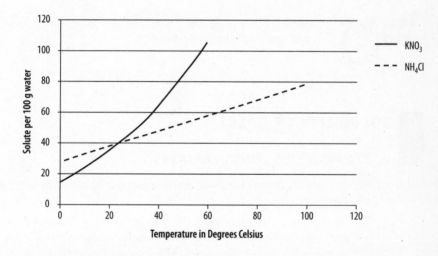

2. When no more solute will dissolve, the solution is said to be *saturated*.
3. Up to the point of saturation, i.e., when it is still possible for more solute to be dissolved, the solution is said to be *unsaturated*.
4. When conditions of temperature or pressure are artificially altered, it may be possible to dissolve more solute than one would otherwise expect in the solvent, i.e., to go beyond the

point of saturation. When this happens, the solution is said to be *supersaturated*.

B. PARTICLE SIZE CONSIDERATIONS

1. Although particle size will influence the SPEED of a solid dissolving, it is not responsible for determining whether a solid will (or will not) dissolve. In that respect, particle size does not affect solubility.

C. AGITATION (STIRRING) CONSIDERATIONS

1. As in particle size considerations, agitation will influence the speed of dissolving but not the amount of solute that will dissolve. In that respect, particle size does not affect solubility.

Test Tip

There is a difference between how MUCH solute can dissolve and how FAST the solute dissolves.

II. SOLUBILITY OF GASES

A. TEMPERATURE CONSIDERATIONS

1. In general, gases become decreasingly soluble with increased temperature.
2. As temperature increases, the gas particles gain energy and can leave the solution more easily, meaning that less of the gas will be dissolved in the solvent and that the concentration of gas in solution will be lower.

B. PRESSURE CONSIDERATIONS

1. In general, gases become increasingly soluble with increased pressure.
2. As pressure increases, more gas particles strike the surface of the solvent and enter the solution, meaning that more

gas is dissolved and that the concentration of the gas in solution will be higher.

3. Henry's law states that at constant temperature and with a constant mass of gas, solubility is directly proportional to pressure.

    i. $\dfrac{S}{P} =$ a constant

    ii. If the solubility and pressure of a gas are known initially, and one of the variables is changed, then the new conditions can be calculated by using $\dfrac{S_1}{P_1} = \dfrac{S_2}{P_2}$.

    (S_1 and P_1 are the original conditions and S_2 and P_2 are the new conditions. Units of solubility and pressure must be the same on each side of the equation.)

Test Tip

Think about a bottle of soda (a fizzy drink). When is the soda most "fizzy," i.e., when does it have most carbon dioxide gas bubbles dissolved in it? It will be most fizzy when it is cold and under pressure. When it is warm and opened (no longer under pressure) the gas is least soluble in the drink and it escapes, making the drink "flat." That's a summary of Henry's law!

QUALITATIVE AND QUANTITATIVE ASPECTS OF COLLIGATIVE PROPERTIES

I. COLLIGATIVE PROPERTIES AND NONELECTROLYTE SOLUTIONS

▶ Colligative properties are properties that are dependent upon the number of particles present and not their nature.

▶ A nonelectrolyte solution is one where the solute particles do not dissociate to any degree when they are dissolved in the solvent, i.e., a nonionic (covalent or molecular) solute.

▶ There are four colligative properties that you need to be familiar with: vapor pressure lowering, boiling point elevation, freezing point depression, and osmotic pressure.

A. VAPOR PRESSURE LOWERING

1. At a given temperature, a pure liquid in a closed container will establish equilibrium with its own vapor.

2. At this point, the pressure created above the liquid is called its *vapor pressure*.

3. The vapor pressure of the pure solvent is lowered when a solute is added, so the vapor pressure above a *solution* is always lower than the vapor pressure above the *pure solvent*.

4. There are two ways to explain why the vapor pressure is lowered when a solute is added.

   i. A simple, physical explanation: When solute particles are introduced, the process of the solvent molecules escaping is partially blocked by the solute particles at the surface, and the vapor pressure falls.

      ii. A more complicated, entropy-based explanation: When a solute is added to a pure solvent, the entropy (disorder) dramatically increases. This is the preferred situation.

5. Changes related to lowering of vapor pressure are governed by *Raoult's law*, and fall into two categories.

      i. Category 1: where the solute is nonvolatile, i.e., those where only the solvent is volatile, Raoult's law states the following:

vapor pressure $= (X) (P°)$

where X = mole fraction

of the solvent $= \dfrac{\text{moles of solvent}}{\text{total number of moles}}$

and

$P°$ = vapor pressure of the pure solvent.

      ii. Category 2: where the solute is also volatile, i.e., those where the solvent AND solute are both volatile.

6. As before, at a fixed temperature, the vapor pressure of each component in the mixture is proportional to the mole fraction of that component so the same equation can be applied, except in these situations you must calculate the vapor pressures for both the solute AND solvent using the equation. Because of Dalton's law, for a mixture of two miscible liquids that obey Raoult's law (see #7 below), you can calculate the total vapor pressure by simply adding the individual vapor pressures.

7. Ideal mixtures are those that obey Raoult's law and are not always found. Nonideal mixtures show deviations from this simple model.

8. In a two-component mixture (where the solute and solvent are both volatile), the vapor above the mixture will always be richer in the lower boiling point component. Lower boiling points mean that liquids can more easily vaporize, so they will produce relatively high vapor pressures when compared to liquids with higher boiling points that vaporize less easily.

B. BOILING POINT ELEVATION

1. The boiling point of a solution is the temperature when the vapor pressure of the solution is equal to the external atmospheric pressure.

2. Because atmospheric pressures are higher than the vapor pressures above solutions, it is necessary to heat the solution in order to increase its vapor pressure to bring it up to the external atmospheric pressure and therefore make the solution boil.

3. Because the addition of a solute lowers the vapor pressure of a solution, it must, by definition, require more energy to be added in order to increase its value to reach the external atmospheric pressure and boil. As a result, the boiling point is raised.

4. For nonelectrolyte solutions, the change in boiling point can be calculated using the following expression:

$$\Delta T_b = K_b\, m$$

In this expression, ΔT_b = change in boiling point of the solvent, K_b = molal boiling point constant for the solvent, and m = molality of the solute = $\dfrac{\text{moles of solute}}{\text{mass of solvent in kg}}$.

Test Tip

The expression for molality is often expanded to introduce the variable, molar mass. The molality expression then becomes

$$m = \dfrac{\dfrac{\text{mass of solute}}{\text{molar mass of solute}}}{\text{mass of solvent in kg}},$$

and questions may ask you to calculate the molar mass.

C. FREEZING POINT DEPRESSION

1. Freezing points are lowered by the addition of nonvolatile solutes. This can be explained in one of two ways.
    i. A simple, physical explanation that involves solute particles actually getting in the way of the

solid structure being formed: If the solidification (freezing) process is hindered, more heat must be removed from the solution, and therefore the freezing point is lowered.

    ii. A more complicated, entropy-based explanation: When the solution has more disorder than the pure solvent, it needs more energy removed from it in order to create the more ordered solid.

2. For *nonelectrolyte solutions*, the change in freezing point can be calculated using the following expression:

$$\Delta T_f = K_f\, m$$

In this expression, ΔT_f = change in freezing point of the solvent, K_f = molal freezing point constant of the solvent, and m = molality of the solute = $\dfrac{\text{moles of solute}}{\text{mass of solvent in kg}}$.

D. OSMOTIC PRESSURE

1. Osmosis is the selective passage of solvent molecules through a porous semipermeable membrane (SPM) from a dilute solution to one of a higher concentration. The SPM allows the passage of solvent but not the passage of solute.

2. The osmotic pressure (π) is the pressure that must be applied in order to prevent osmosis from occurring.

3. For *nonelectrolyte solutions*, the osmotic pressure can be calculated by using the following expression:

$$\pi = MRT$$

In this expression, M = molarity, R = universal gas constant (0.0821 L atm mol^{-1} K^{-1}), and T = temperature in Kelvin.

II. COLLIGATIVE PROPERTIES AND ELECTROLYTE SOLUTIONS

A. THE VAN'T HOFF FACTOR

1. Electrolytes require a slightly different approach than nonelectrolyte solutions because they dissociate in solution

and provide a greater number of solute particles than the undissolved solute.

2. Because colligative properties depend on the number of particles present, you must take this dissociation into account.

3. For example, one formula unit of $MgCl_2$ splits into three particles when it is dissolved in solution (one $Mg^{2+}_{(aq)}$ ion and two $Cl^-_{(aq)}$ ions). This should produce a freezing point depression three times greater than a nonelectrolyte solute that does not produce a greater number of particles when dissolved; for example, molecular, nonionic sucrose, $C_6H_{12}O_6$.

4. In order to account for this, the van't Hoff factor (i) is added to the preceding equations.

   i. Boiling point elevation:

   $$\Delta T_b = i K_b m$$

   ii. Freezing point depression:

   $$\Delta T_f = i K_f m$$

   iii. Osmotic pressure:

   $$\pi = i MRT$$

   iv. In each case, the van't Hoff factor is given as:

   $$i = \frac{\text{actual number of particles in solution after d}}{\text{d} \qquad \text{dissociation}}$$

   v. For nonelectrolytes, i = 1 (because they do not dissociate).

   vi. Electrolytes usually have a van't Hoff factor that is slightly less than the predicted one. For example, $MgCl_2$ has i = 2.7 rather than the predicted 3.0, due to the pairing of some of the ions in solution. The pairing of ions is most prevalent when the ions involved have higher charges, and the solution is relatively concentrated.

Test Tip

If a question refers to a molecular, covalent, nonionic, or nonconducting solution, it means that the solution does not contain ions, the solute does not dissociate, and therefore i = 1.

PART IV:

REACTION TYPES

ACIDS AND BASES: BRØNSTED-LOWRY THEORY AND OTHER DEFINITIONS OF ACIDS AND BASES

I. BRØNSTED-LOWRY ACIDS AND BASES

A. THE BRØNSTED-LOWRY THEORY IS ONE METHOD OF CLASSIFYING ACIDS AND BASES

1. An acid is defined as a proton (hydrogen ion, H^+) donor.

2. A base is defined as a proton (hydrogen ion, H^+) acceptor.

3. Example #1. In the following reaction, HCl acts as an acid because it gives H^+ to H_2O, and H_2O acts as a base because it accepts the H^+ ion from HCl to form H_3O^+.

$$HCl_{(aq)} + H_2O_{(l)} \rightarrow H_3O^+_{(aq)} + Cl^-_{(aq)}$$

4. Example #2. In the following reaction, H_2O acts as an acid because it gives H^+ to NH_3, and NH_3 acts as a base because it accepts the H^+ ion from H_2O to form NH_4^+.

$$NH_{3(aq)} + H_2O_{(l)} \rightarrow NH_4^+_{(aq)} + OH^-_{(aq)}$$

B. BRØNSTED ACID AND BASE CONJUGATE PAIRS

1. Conjugate acid and base pairs are related to one another by a difference of H^+ on either side of the equation, where the conjugate acid has one more H^+ than its corresponding conjugate base.

2. Example #1. In the following reaction, HCl and Cl^- are a conjugate acid–base pair, where HCl is the acid and Cl^- is the base. Similarly, H_3O^+ and H_2O can be considered to be an acid–base conjugate pair as well, with H_3O^+ being the acid and H_2O the base.

$$HCl_{(aq)} + H_2O_{(l)} \rightarrow H_3O^+_{(aq)} + Cl^-_{(aq)}$$

3. Example #2. In the following reaction, H_2O and OH^- are a conjugate acid–base pair, where H_2O is the acid and OH^- is the base. Similarly, NH_4^+ and NH_3 can be considered to be an acid–base conjugate pair as well, with NH_4^+ being the acid and NH_3 the base.

$$NH_{3(aq)} + H_2O_{(l)} \rightarrow NH_4^+{}_{(aq)} + OH^-{}_{(aq)}$$

II. OTHER DEFINITIONS OF ACIDS AND BASES

A. LEWIS ACIDS AND BASES

1. An acid is defined as an electron pair acceptor.
2. A base is defined as an electron pair donor.
3. Example. In the following reaction, the electron-rich nitrogen atom in NH_3 acts as a Lewis base by donating a pair of electrons to the electron-deficient boron atom in BF_3. In turn, the boron atom acts as a Lewis acid by accepting the pair of electrons from the nitrogen atom. As a result, a dative (or coordinate) bond is formed.

$$:NH_3 + BF_3 \rightarrow H_3N{:}{\rightarrow}BF_3$$

In order to recognize electron-rich and electron-deficient species, and therefore which species might act as Lewis acids and Lewis bases, you must be able to draw and understand Lewis diagrams. This is an example of needing to see links between the different topic areas of your course, and not to always consider them in isolation. The most successful students always try to find the common ground between topic areas.

B. ARRHENIUS ACIDS AND BASES

1. An acid is defined as a substance that dissolves in water to produce H^+ (H_3O^+) ions. (See the Test Tip.)

Acids are defined as H^+ donors, but be aware that they are sometimes written in equations where water is present, and sometimes written in equations where no water is present. For example, hydrochloric acid, HCl, can be shown as:

$$HCl \rightarrow H^+ + Cl^-$$
or as,
$$HCl + H_2O \rightarrow H_3O^+ + Cl^-$$

That is, HCl can be shown with one equation simply showing the formation of H^+ with no water present, and in another equation showing H_2O and the subsequent formation of H_3O^+. As a result, H^+ and H_3O^+ on the product side of the equation are often thought of as being interchangeable and equivalent. Look out for this and be aware that, in this context, they mean the same thing!

2. A base is defined as a substance that dissolves in water to produce OH^- (hydroxide) ions.

3. Example #1. In the following reaction, HCl acts as an acid because it produces the H^+ ions that combine with water to produce H_3O^+ in solution.

$$HCl_{(aq)} + H_2O_{(l)} \rightarrow H_3O^+_{(aq)} + Cl^-_{(aq)}$$

(HCl is also acting as an acid in terms of the Brønsted-Lowry definition.)

4. Example #2. In the following reaction, NH_3 acts as a base because via its reaction with water, it produces OH^- in solution.

$$NH_{3(aq)} + H_2O_{(l)} \rightarrow NH_4^+_{(aq)} + OH^-_{(aq)}$$

(NH_3 is also acting as a base in terms of the Brønsted-Lowry definition.)

STRONG AND WEAK ACIDS AND BASES, pH, AND BUFFERS

I. STRENGTH OF ACIDS AND BASES

A. DEGREE OF IONIZATION

1. Strong acids and strong bases exhibit complete ionization (dissociation).
2. For a strong acid (e.g., HCl) and a strong base (e.g., NaOH) the following reactions go to completion (ionization is considered to be 100% with no reverse reaction), to produce large numbers of $H_3O^+_{(aq)}$ and $OH^-_{(aq)}$, respectively.

$$HCl_{(aq)} + H_2O_{(l)} \rightarrow H_3O^+_{(aq)} + Cl^-_{(aq)}$$
$$NaOH_{(aq)} \rightarrow Na^+_{(aq)} + OH^-_{(aq)}$$

3. For a weak acid (e.g., CH_3COOH) and a weak base (e.g., NH_3) the following reactions do *not* go to completion (ionization is considered to be very small, perhaps 5% or less, with a reverse reaction that sets up an equilibrium), to produce small numbers of $H_3O^+_{(aq)}$ and $OH^-_{(aq)}$, respectively.

$$CH_3COOH_{(aq)} + H_2O_{(l)} \rightleftarrows H_3O^+_{(aq)} + CH_3COO^-_{(aq)}$$
$$NH_{3(aq)} + H_2O_{(l)} \rightleftarrows NH_4^+_{(aq)} + OH^-_{(aq)}$$

4. Examples of weak acids include organic (carboxylic) acids, e.g., methanoic acid (HCOOH), ethanoic acid (CH_3COOH), and propanoic acid (C_2H_5COOH).
5. Examples of strong acids include inorganic (mineral) acids, e.g., hydrochloric acid (HCl), sulfuric acid (H_2SO_4), and nitric acid (HNO_3).

6. Examples of weak bases include ammonia (NH_3) and organic bases, e.g., methylamine (CH_3NH_2) and ethylamine ($C_2H_5NH_2$).

7. Examples of strong bases include inorganic bases, e.g., sodium hydroxide (NaOH), potassium hydroxide (KOH), and calcium hydroxide ($Ca(OH)_2$).

B. pH SCALE

1. The pH scale is used to indicate how acidic or a basic a substance is.

2. pH ranges from 0–14. Acids have a pH of less than 7, bases have a pH of greater than 7, and 7 on the scale is considered to be neutral.

3. pH is defined as the following:

$$pH = -\log[H_3O^+] \quad \text{or} \quad pH = -\log[H^+]$$

4. For strong acids that completely dissociate, because the concentration of the hydrogen ions will be the same as the concentration of the acid, simply take the $-\log$ of the concentration of the acid to yield the pH.

    i. For example, calculate the pH of a 0.01 M solution of HCl.

$$HCl_{(aq)} + H_2O_{(l)} \rightarrow H_3O^+{}_{(aq)} + Cl^-{}_{(aq)}$$

0.01   0.01

$$pH = -\log(0.01) = 2.00$$

Test Tip

Because of the math of the pH expression, a change by a factor of 10 in the hydrogen ion concentration will result in a difference of 1 pH unit. For example, $-\log(0.1) = 1$, $-\log(0.01) = 2$, $-\log(0.001) = 3$, and so on.

Another useful math tip is to know that if the hydrogen ion concentration is expressed in scientific form—e.g., 1×10^{-1}—then the pH will be equal to the absolute value of the power, in this case, pH = 1.

5. Weak acids are not completely dissociated and require the use of Ka (the acid dissociation constant) in order to calculate pH.

6. Other ways to calculate pH include the following.

    i. Because bases produce hydroxide ions in solution, the pOH can be calculated as follows.

$$pOH = -\log[OH^-]$$

    ii. At 298 K, the relationship between pH and pOH is given as the following.

$$pH + pOH = 14$$

II. Ka—THE EQUILIBRIUM CONSTANT FOR WEAK ACIDS

A. INCOMPLETE IONIZATION AND EQUILIBRIA

1. For a weak acid, dissociation is incomplete and an equilibrium exists.

2. You can set up an ICE table (one that summarizes **I**nitial conditions, **C**hanges in conditions, and **E**quilibrium conditions) to illustrate the reversible reaction of a weak acid, HA, with water.

ICE Table

$HA_{(aq)} + H_2O_{(l)} \rightleftarrows H_3O^+_{(aq)} + A^-_{(aq)}$		
Initial	C	0	0
Change	$-x$	$+x$	$+x$
Equilibrium	$C - x$	$0 + x$	$0 + x$

    i. The acid starts with a concentration of C and dissociates into ions.

    ii. Because it is a weak acid, it does not completely dissociate so it is not possible to go directly to $pH = -\log[C]$.

    iii. However, we do know that because the acid is weak, and there is very little dissociation, x will be small and can be considered negligible in the term C-x.

iv. Additionally, because of the 1:1 ratio we know that the concentrations of $H_3O^+_{(aq)}$ and $A^-_{(aq)}$ will be equal.

v. Considering those facts, and knowing that $H_2O_{(l)}$ is a pure liquid and like all pure liquids and solids it will not appear in the equilibrium expression, you can derive the following.

a) Ka, the acid dissociation constant, like all equilibrium constants, has the concentrations of the products placed in the numerator and multiplied together, and the concentrations of the reactants placed in the denominator and multiplied together, as shown in the following equations for this case.

$$Ka = \frac{[H_3O^+][A^-]}{[HA]}$$

or,

$$Ka = \frac{[H_3O^+]^2}{[HA]}$$

b) pKa: A mathematically useful relationship is, pKa = −log Ka.

Test Tip

Even within weak acids, there is a hierarchy of strength. Because the strength of an acid is determined by its ability to dissociate and produce H^+ (H_3O^+) ions, and those ions appear in the numerator of the Ka expression, the larger the Ka, the stronger the (weak) acid. However, taking the negative log of the Ka gives pKa, and by means of math we find that the larger the Ka, the smaller the pKa. In summary, the stronger the weak acid, the larger the Ka. The larger the Ka, the smaller the pKa.

III. Kb—THE EQUILIBRIUM CONSTANT FOR WEAK BASES

A. INCOMPLETE IONIZATION AND EQUILIBRIA

1. For a weak base, dissociation is incomplete and an equilibrium exists.
2. You can set up an ICE table (one that summarizes **I**nitial conditions, **C**hanges in conditions, and **E**quilibrium conditions) to illustrate the reversible reaction of a weak base with water. For example, reaction of ammonia, NH_3 with water is shown in the following ICE table.

ICE Table

	$NH_{3(aq)} + H_2O_{(l)} \rightleftarrows NH_4^+{}_{(aq)} + OH^-{}_{(aq)}$		
Initial	C	0	0
Change	−x	+x	+x
Equilibrium	C − x	0 + x	0 + x

  i. The base starts with a concentration of C and dissociates into ions.
  ii. Because it is a weak base, it does not completely dissociate, so it is not possible to go directly to $pOH = -\log [C]$.
  iii. However, we do know that because the base is weak, and there is very little dissociation, x will be small and can be considered negligible in the term C-x.
  iv. Additionally, because of 1:1 ratio we know that the concentrations of $NH_4^+{}_{(aq)}$ and $OH^-{}_{(aq)}$ will be equal.
  v. Considering those facts, and knowing that $H_2O_{(l)}$ is a pure liquid, and, like all pure liquids and solids, it will not appear in the equilibrium expression, you can derive the following.
   a) Kb, the base dissociation constant, like all equilibrium constants, has the concentrations of the products placed in the numerator and multiplied together, and the concentrations of the reactants placed in the denominator and

multiplied together, as shown in the following equations for this case.

$$Kb = \frac{[OH^-][NH_4^+]}{[NH_3]}$$

or,

$$Kb = \frac{[OH^-]^2}{[NH_3]}$$

b) pKb: A mathematically useful relationship is pKb = −log Kb (See previous Test Tip to understand relative sizes of Kb and pKb and their relationship to strength [p. 108].).

IV. Kw—THE IONIC PRODUCT OF WATER

A. THE SELF-IONIZATION OF WATER

1. Although pure water is essentially covalent, there is a small amount of self-ionization that occurs.

$$H_2O_{(l)} + H_2O_{(l)} \rightleftarrows H_3O^+_{(aq)} + OH^-_{(aq)}$$

2. Another equilibrium constant, Kw, can be derived as such: Kw = $[H_3O^+][OH^-]$.

3. As any equilibrium constant, Kw is temperature dependent. At 298 K, Kw = 1×10^{-14} and pKw = −log Kw = 14.

4. Because pure H_2O will have equal concentrations of $H_3O^+_{(aq)}$ and $OH^-_{(aq)}$, then under these conditions, $[H_3O^+_{(aq)}]$ = $[OH^-_{(aq)}]$ = $\sqrt{1 \times 10^{-14}}$ = 1×10^{-7}. Applying pH = −log $[H_3O^+_{(aq)}]$, we find that the pH of pure water at 298 K is 7, i.e., it is neutral.

Test Tip *Another useful relationship is that for an acid–base conjugate pair, Kw = (Ka) (Kb).*

V. POLYPROTIC ACIDS

A. POLYPROTIC ACIDS AND EQUILIBRIUM CONSTANTS

1. Polyprotic acids have more than 1 hydrogen ion that they can donate in acid–base reactions.

2. Hydrogen ions are donated, one at a time, in individual steps. For example, carbonic acid can donate a total of 2 hydrogen ions to water in single steps, where the species formed becomes the "new" acid in the subsequent step.

   Step 1:

   $$H_2CO_{3(aq)} + H_2O_{(l)} \rightleftarrows H_3O^+_{(aq)} + HCO_3^-_{(aq)}$$

   Step 2:

   $$HCO_3^-_{(aq)} + H_2O_{(l)} \rightleftarrows H_3O^+_{(aq)} + CO_3^{2-}_{(aq)}$$

   Overall:

   $$H_2CO_{3(aq)} + 2H_2O_{(l)} \rightleftarrows 2H_3O^+_{(aq)} + CO_3^{2-}_{(aq)}$$

3. In such cases, in each step, the acid can either be strong or weak. Any weak acids can have their own, individual Ka expressions.

   Step 1:

   $$Ka = \frac{[H_3O^+][HCO_3^-]}{[H_2CO_3]},$$

   Step 2:

   $$Ka = \frac{[H_3O^+][CO_3^{2-}]}{[HCO_3^-]},$$

   Overall:

   $$Ka = \frac{[H_3O^+]^2[CO_3^{2-}]}{[H_2CO_3]}$$

   Inspection shows that Ka (overall) = (Ka (step 1)) (Ka (step 2)), and this is true of all multiple, simultaneous equilibria.

VI. BUFFER SOLUTIONS

A. DEFINITION

1. A buffer solution is one that resists changes in pH when either a small amount of acid or base is added to it.

B. COMPOSITION AND ACTION

1. Usually, a buffer solution is made from a weak acid and its conjugate base (which is one of its salts), or a weak base and its conjugate acid (which is one of its salts). For example, a combination of ethanoic acid and sodium ethanoate solutions make a buffer.

2. The ethanoate ions will be able to absorb any excess acid that is added.

$$CH_3CO_2^- + H_3O^+ \rightarrow CH_3CO_2H + H_2O$$

3. The ethanoic acid will be able to absorb any excess base that is added.

$$CH_3CO_2H + OH^- \rightarrow CH_3CO_2^- + H_2O$$

C. pH OF BUFFERS

1. To calculate the pH of an acidic buffer, use

$$pH = pKa + \log \frac{[salt]}{[acid]} .$$

2. To calculate the pH of a basic buffer, use

$$pOH = pKb + \log \frac{[salt]}{[base]} .$$

TITRATIONS AND INDICATORS

I. INDICATORS

A. THE NATURE OF INDICATORS

1. An acid–base indicator is a substance that changes color according to the pH of the solution.
2. In practice, the indicator will change color over a small, given range of pH.

B. EXAMPLES OF INDICATORS

Some Common Indicators and the pH Range Over Which They Change Color

	Color in Acid	Approximate pH Range of Color Change Takes Place	Color in Base
Methyl Orange	Red	3–5	Yellow
Methyl Red	Red	4–6	Yellow
Litmus	Red	5–8	Blue
Phenolphthalein	Colorless	9–10	Pink

Test Tip

It is worth knowing a few of the common indicators listed in the common indicators table, along with the pH ranges over which they change color and their colors in acid and base solution.

TITRATIONS

A. PRINCIPLES

1. A *titration* is a method of quantitatively analyzing a solution of unknown concentration, by reacting it with a solution of known concentration.

2. A *primary standard* is a solution whose concentration is accurately known.

   i. A mass of a solid (the solute) is accurately weighed and transferred carefully to a volumetric flask.

   ii. The solid is then dissolved in a small amount of water (the solvent) and the solution made up to a specific volume.

   iii. Solids used as primary standards must be pure, must dissolve in water easily, should not decompose, and should have a relatively high molecular mass.

B. PROCEDURE

1. When filling the burette, wash it through with some of the solution first and then carefully fill it.

2. When using the pipette, wash it through with some of the solution first and then carefully fill it using a safety pipette filler. You can then transfer the solution to an Erlenmeyer flask ready for titration.

3. When performing the titration, use the following guidelines.

   i. You can add a few drops of indicator to the Erlenmeyer flask, and place the flask underneath the burette. A white background is useful to aid the observation of the indicator color change.

   ii. Having noted the initial volume, run the solution in the burette into the flask a few milliliters at a time, each time swirling the flask gently.

   iii. As you approach the end point, add the burette solution dropwise. Note the final volume. Read the burette to 0.05 mL and perform a number of titrations until you reach concordance.

C. CHOICE OF INDICATOR AND TITRATION CURVES

1. The following titration curves can be plotted from data.

Titration Curves

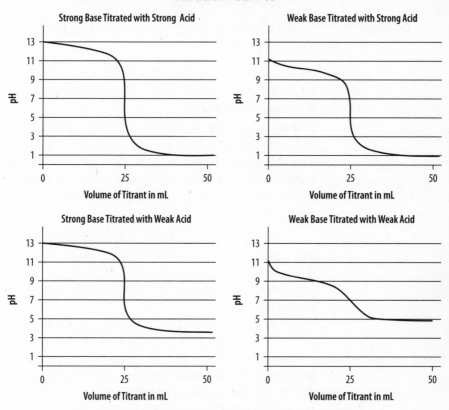

2. The equivalence point represents the point at which stoichiometrically equal amounts of acid and base have reacted, and is located in the middle of the vertical portion of the titration curve.

Test Tip

"End point" (the point at which the indicator changes color) and equivalence point *have subtley different meanings. Understand the difference.*

3. Because, in an acid–base titration we need to find the equivalence point, we must choose an indicator that changes color over a pH range as close to equivalence point as possible.

4. For a weak acid–weak base titration, there is no sharp change in pH at the equivalence point, so no indicator will change color sharply at the equivalence point. Another method such as the use of a pH meter must be used in such titrations.

D. HYDROLYSIS OF SALTS AND WHY pH IS NOT ALWAYS 7 AT THE EQUIVALENCE POINT

1. Careful analysis of titration curves shows that the equivalence point is not necessarily at pH 7. This is due to the hydrolysis reaction of the salts produced.

   i. In a strong acid/strong base titration where the pH is 7, no hydrolysis occurs.

   ii. In a strong base/weak acid titration where the pH is greater than 7, the conjugate base of the weak acid yields OH^- ions in solution. See the following example.

   $$CH_3COO^- + H_2O \rightleftarrows CH_3COOH + OH^-$$

   iii. In a strong acid/weak base titration where the pH is less than 7, the conjugate acid of the weak base yields H_3O^+ ions in solution. See the following example.

   $$NH_4^+ + H_2O \rightleftarrows NH_3 + H_3O^+$$

   iv. In a weak acid/weak base titration where various pH's are possible, if Kb for the anion is greater than Ka for the cation, then pH will be BASIC. If Ka for the cation is greater than Kb for the anion, then the pH will be ACIDIC. If Ka is approximately equal to Kb, then the pH will be NEUTRAL.

Test Tip

An easy way to remember these patterns is that "strong always wins," meaning that when a strong acid or base is matched with a weak acid or base, the pH at the equivalence point will always favor the stronger component.

E. POLYPROTIC ACIDS AND TITRATION CURVES

1. Polyprotic acids have more than 1 hydrogen ion that they can donate in acid–base reactions.

2. Hydrogen ions are donated, one at a time, in individual steps. For example, phosphoric acid can donate a total of 3 hydrogen ions to water in single steps, and each time the species formed becomes the "new" acid in the subsequent step.

$$H_3PO_4 + H_2O \rightarrow H_2PO_4^- + H_3O^+$$
$$H_2PO_4^- + H_2O \rightarrow HPO_4^{2-} + H_3O^+$$
$$HPO_4^{2-} + H_2O \rightarrow PO_4^{3-} + H_3O^+$$

3. In such cases, in each step, the acid can either be strong or weak and in each case it has its own equivalence point. As a result, you can construct titration curves with multiple equivalence points. See the following diagram.

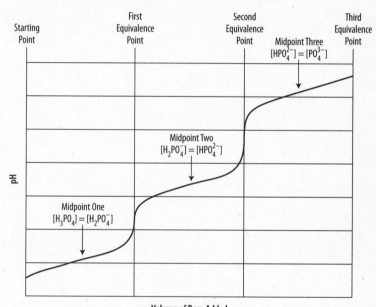

Volume of Base Added

During titrations involving weak acids or weak bases, solutions that contain the acid or base, plus its conjugate base or acid, are produced in the flask. These are buffer solutions (see Chapter 19). At the midpoint to any equivalence point, the concentration of the acid or base and its corresponding conjugate salt will be equal and at this point pH = pKa. Because an equal concentration of both components means that the buffer solution can absorb acid and base equally well, these solutions are considered to be the most effective buffers. Look out for questions that highlight situations that are midpoint to equivalence points, and link that to buffers.

OXIDATION NUMBERS AND **REDOX**

I. OXIDATION NUMBER CONCEPT

A. DEFINITION

1. Oxidation number is the number of electrons that an atom loses or gains, when it forms a new substance.
2. If the atom gains, or tends to gain, electrons, then the oxidation number is negative.
3. If the atom loses, or tends to lose, electrons, then the oxidation number is positive.
4. In the case of covalent compounds, the oxidation number is regarded as the charge the species *would* develop *if* the compound were fully ionic.
5. Following are the oxidation number rules:
    i. The oxidation number of an element when uncombined (as the free element) is always zero.
    ii. The sum of the oxidation numbers in a neutral substance is always zero.
    iii. In an ion, the sum of the oxidation numbers equals the ionic charge.
    iv. Some elements exhibit very common oxidation numbers in their compounds.
        a) Group 1 elements are always $+1$, group 2 elements are always $+2$, F is always -1, O is *almost* always -2, and H is *almost* always $+1$.
        b) In binary compounds with metals, the group 17 elements are -1, the group 16 elements are -2, and the group 15 elements are -3.

6. For example, calculate the oxidation number of Cr in $K_2Cr_2O_7$ by applying rules.

$K = (2)(+1) = +2$ (group 1 is always $+1$)

$Cr = (2)(x) = 2x$ (x is the unknown oxidation number of Cr)

$O = (7)(-2) = -14$ (O is *almost* always -2)

Sum of the oxidation numbers $= 0$ (rule 5ii.)

$0 = +2 + 2x + -14$, so $x = +6$

II. OXIDATION AND REDUCTION REACTIONS

A. DEFINITION OF REDOX

1. Oxidation and reduction can be defined in a number of ways, one of which is in terms of electrons.
2. Oxidation is defined as a LOSS of electrons.
3. Reduction is defined as a GAIN of electrons.

Test Tip

Remember the mnemonics, OILRIG (oxidation is loss, reduction is gain) or LEO GER (losing electrons oxidation, gaining electrons reduction).

4. An *oxidizing agent* is one that causes oxidation; i.e., it causes another species to become oxidized. Oxidizing agents do this by accepting electrons, and in the process *they* become reduced.
5. A *reducing agent* is one that causes reduction; i.e., it causes another species to become reduced. Reducing agents do this by donating electrons, and in the process *they* become oxidized.
6. For example, consider the formation of sodium bromide from its elements.

$$2Na + Br_2 \rightarrow 2NaBr$$

This complete reaction can be thought of as two half equations, one involving oxidation and one involving reduction. Half equations include electrons.

  i. Oxidation (electrons are lost):

$$Na \rightarrow Na^+ + e^-$$

  ii. Reduction (electrons are gained):

$$Br_2 + 2e^- \rightarrow 2Br^-$$

  iii. When combining two half equations, it is necessary to cancel out the electrons in order to produce the full, balanced, REDOX equation. In this case, multiply the oxidation half equation by 2 and merge with the reduction half equation to yield the full REDOX equation.

$$2Na + Br_2 \rightarrow 2NaBr$$

Test Tip

Unlike half equations that show the individual processes of oxidation and reduction, full REDOX equations should NOT contain electrons, so be sure to check that the electrons have been canceled out in the full REDOX equation.

B. REDOX REACTIONS IN ACID AND BASE SOLUTION

1. Sometimes, when more complicated species are present, a half equation can be more difficult to write, usually when oxygen is present in a polyatomic ion or compound.
2. When this occurs, the equation can be balanced with H^+ ions (acid), OH^- ions (base), and/or water.
3. When balancing "in acid," use water, H^+, and electrons.
4. When balancing "in base," balance in acid solution FIRST (using water, H^+, and electrons), and then add hydroxide (OH^-) ions to each side of the equation to remove excess H^+. Cancel and tidy as necessary.

5. For example, "in acid," MnO_4^- is a strong oxidizing agent that is converted to Mn^{2+}.

    i. The equation starts as:

$$MnO_4^- \rightarrow Mn^{2+}$$

    ii. Add $4H_2O$ to the right-hand side to balance the O atoms.

$$MnO_4^- \rightarrow Mn^{2+} + \mathbf{4H_2O}$$

    iii. Add $8H^+$ to the left-hand side to balance the H atoms.

$$MnO_4^- + \mathbf{8H^+} \rightarrow Mn^{2+} + 4H_2O$$

    iv. Add $5e^-$ to the left-hand side to balance the charge.

$$MnO_4^- + 8H^+ + \mathbf{5e^-} \rightarrow Mn^{2+} + 4H_2O$$

6. For example, "in base," MnO_4^- is a strong oxidizing agent that is converted to MnO_2.

    i. The equation starts as:

$$MnO_4^- \rightarrow MnO_2$$

    ii. Add $2H_2O$ to the right-hand side to balance the O atoms.

$$MnO_4^- \rightarrow MnO_2 + \mathbf{2H_2O}$$

    iii. Add $4H^+$ to the left-hand side to balance the H atoms.

$$MnO_4^- + \mathbf{4H^+} \rightarrow MnO_2 + 2H_2O$$

    iv. Add $3e^-$ to the left-hand side to balance the charge.

$$MnO_4^- + 4H^+ + \mathbf{3e^-} \rightarrow MnO_2 + 2H_2O$$

v. Add OH⁻ to both sides in order to neutralize the acid (H⁺). (It must be added to both sides because in iv., the equation was already balanced.)

$$MnO_4^- + 4H^+ + 3e^- + 4OH^- \rightarrow MnO_2 + 2H_2O + 4OH^-$$

vi. "Tidy" the equation by combining H⁺ and OH⁻ to make water on the left-hand side, and then canceling water molecules as required.

$$MnO_4^- + 3e^- + 2H_2O \rightarrow MnO_2 + 4OH^-$$

Test Tip

When writing both half reactions and full REDOX equations, be careful to balance both the atoms AND the charges.

C. COMMON OXIDIZING AND REDUCING AGENTS

1. *Oxidizing agents.* These reagents allow the species with which they come into contact to lose electrons. They do this by readily accepting those electrons.

   i. In general, nonmetals tend to be oxidizing agents because they want to gain electrons. See the following examples.

   $$F_2 + 2e^- \rightarrow 2F^-$$
   $$Cl_2 + 2e^- \rightarrow 2Cl^-$$
   $$O_2 + 4H^+ + 4e^- \rightarrow 2H_2O$$

   ii. Oxyanions and some compounds of transition metals also commonly act as oxidizing agents. See the following examples.

   $$MnO_4^- + 8H^+ + 5e^- \rightarrow Mn^{2+} + 4H_2O$$
   $$Cr_2O_7^{2-} + 14H^+ + 6e^- \rightarrow 2Cr^{3+} + 7H_2O$$
   $$MnO_2 + 4H^+ + 2e^- \rightarrow Mn^{2+} + 2H_2O$$

2. *Reducing agents.* These reagents allow the species with which they come into contact to gain electrons. They do this by readily losing (and donating) those electrons.

   i. In general, metals tend to be reducing agents because they want to lose electrons. See the following examples.

$$Na \rightarrow Na^+ + e^-$$

$$Zn \rightarrow Zn^{2+} + 2e^-$$

$$Sn \rightarrow Sn^{2+} + 2e^-$$

REDOX REACTIONS, THE ACTIVITY SERIES AND ELECTROCHEMISTRY

I. CLASSIFYING REDOX REACTIONS

A. DISPROPORTIONATION

1. *Disproportionation* is a reaction where there is a simultaneous oxidation and reduction of a single species. See the following example.

$$3ClO^-_{(aq)} \rightarrow ClO_3^-{}_{(aq)} + 2Cl^-_{(aq)}$$

In this reaction, Cl^+ is oxidized to Cl^{5+} and Cl^+ is simultaneously reduced to Cl^-.

B. SYNTHESIS (OR COMBINATION)

1. *Synthesis* (or *combination*) is a reaction where a compound is formed by the reaction of simpler materials, often its elements. See the following example.

$$2H_{2(g)} + O_{2(g)} \rightarrow 2H_2O_{(l)}$$

In this reaction, H^0 is oxidized to H^- and O^0 is reduced to O^{2-}.

C. DECOMPOSITION

1. *Decomposition* is a reaction where a compound is broken down into simpler substances. It is the reverse of a synthesis reaction. See the following example.

$$2HgO_{(s)} \rightarrow 2Hg_{(g)} + O_{2(g)}$$

In this reaction, Hg^{2+} is reduced to Hg^0 and O^{2-} is oxidized to O^0.

D. SINGLE DISPLACEMENT (SINGLE REPLACEMENT)

1. *Single displacement* (or *single replacement*) is a reaction where an atom or ion in a compound is displaced (replaced) by another atom or ion.

   i. Metal displacement is shown in the following example.

   $$Zn_{(s)} + CuSO_{4(aq)} \rightarrow ZnSO_{4(aq)} + Cu_{(s)}$$

   In this reaction, Zn^0 is oxidized to Zn^{2+} and Cu^{2+} is reduced to Cu^0.

   ii. Hydrogen displacement:

   a) Hydrogen displacement from water is shown in the following example.

   $$2Na_{(s)} + 2H_2O_{(l)} \rightarrow 2NaOH_{(aq)} + H_{2(g)}$$

   In this reaction, Na^0 is oxidized to Na^+ and H^+ is reduced to H^0.

   b) Hydrogen displacement from acids is shown in the following example.

   $$Zn_{(s)} + 2HCl_{(aq)} \rightarrow ZnCl_{2(aq)} + H_{2(g)}$$

   In this reaction, Zn^0 is oxidized to Zn^{2+} and H^+ is reduced to H^0.

   The reactions in (i) and (ii) can be replicated using many different metals and solutions but not all combinations result in a reaction. See Activity Series later in this chapter.

   iii. Halogen displacement is shown in the following example.

   $$Cl_{2(g)} + 2KBr_{(aq)} \rightarrow 2KCl_{(aq)} + Br_{2(l)}$$

   In this reaction, Br^- is oxidized to Br^0 and Cl^0 is reduced to Cl^-. Once again, not all combinations lead to a reaction. Some halogens will displace other halogens from solutions of their ions but some will not. A halogen high in group 17 will displace one below it from a solution of its ions, but the reverse is not possible.

E. COMBUSTION

1. *Combustion* is a reaction where a compound or element burns in oxygen. Very often this is a hydrocarbon (a compound of hydrogen and carbon) that reacts with oxygen to form carbon dioxide and water. See the following example.

$$C_3H_{8(g)} + 5O_{2(g)} \rightarrow 3CO_{2(g)} + 4H_2O_{(l)}$$

In this reaction, O^0 is reduced to O^{2-} and carbon and hydrogen gain oxygen and are said to be *oxidized*.

F. REDOX REACTIONS AS GAS-PRODUCING REACTIONS

1. Acid + Metal → Salt + Hydrogen. See the following example.

$$Zn_{(s)} + 2HCl_{(aq)} \rightarrow ZnCl_{2(aq)} + H_{2(g)}$$

In this reaction, zinc is oxidized, and hydrogen is reduced.

    i. A simple lab test for hydrogen is the "squeaky pop" test with lighted splint.

2. Oxygen is produced by the decomposition of hydrogen peroxide with a MnO_2 catalyst. See the following reaction.

$$2H_2O_{2(aq)} \rightarrow 2H_2O_{(l)} + O_{2(g)}$$

In this reaction, is oxygen is both oxidized and reduced.

    i. A simple lab test for oxygen is the relighting of a glowing splint.

Test Tip

Being able to recognize the oxidation states of individual atoms is crucial. It will allow you to quickly identify what is being oxidized and what is being reduced. Practice that skill!

II. ACTIVITY SERIES

A. DISPLACEMENT REACTIONS

1. Some metals will displace other metals from solutions, some will not.
2. Some metals will undergo displacement reactions with water, some with acids, some with both, and some with neither.

3. You can use the activity series to make predictions regarding which metals will (and which will not) undergo the displacement reactions discussed earlier. Metals are arranged in order of increasing ability to displace hydrogen, with the most reactive at the top.

   i. All metals above hydrogen in the series will displace it from an acid.

   ii. All metals below hydrogen will not displace it from an acid or water.

   iii. A metal relatively high in the series will displace one below it from a solution of its ions but the reverse process is not possible.

Activity Series of Metals

Metal	React with Acid?	React with Steam?	React with Cold Water?
K	YES	YES	YES
Na	YES	YES	YES
Li	YES	YES	YES
Ca	YES	YES	YES
Mg	YES	YES	NO
Al	YES	YES	NO
Zn	YES	YES	NO
Fe	YES	YES	NO
Sn	YES	NO	NO
Pb	YES	NO	NO
Hydrogen			
Cu	NO	NO	NO
Ag	NO	NO	NO
Au	NO	NO	NO
Pt	NO	NO	NO

 Make up your own mnemonic to remember the activity series.

III. ELECTROCHEMISTRY

A. STANDARD ELECTRODE REDUCTION POTENTIALS (SERPs)

1. The relative likelihood of a REDOX half equation occurring is summarized in the following standard electrode reduction potential table.

Note: All half equations are shown as reductions.

STANDARD ELECTRODE POTENTIAL IN AQUEOUS SOLUTIONS AT 25°C		
Electrode	**Electrode Reaction**	**$E°_{red}(V)$**
Acid Solutions		
$Li \mid Li^+$	$Li^+ + e^- \rightleftharpoons Li$	−3.045
$K \mid K^+$	$K^+ + e^- \rightleftharpoons K$	−2.925
$Ba \mid Ba^{2+}$	$Ba^{2+} + 2e^- \rightleftharpoons Ba$	−2.906
$Ca \mid Ca^{2+}$	$Ca^{2+} + 2e^- \rightleftharpoons Ca$	−2.87
$Na \mid Na^+$	$Na^+ + e^- \rightleftharpoons Na$	−2.714
$La \mid La^{3+}$	$La^{3+} + 3e^- \rightleftharpoons La$	−2.52
$Mg \mid Mg^{2+}$	$Mg^{2+} + 2e^- \rightleftharpoons Mg$	−2.363
$Th \mid Th^{4+}$	$Th^{4+} + 4e^- \rightleftharpoons Th$	−1.90
$U \mid U^{3+}$	$U^{3+} + 3e^- \rightleftharpoons U$	−1.80
$Al \mid Al^{3+}$	$Al^{3+} + 3e^- \rightleftharpoons Al$	−1.66
$Mn \mid Mn^{2+}$	$Mn^{2+} + 2e^- \rightleftharpoons Mn$	−1.180
$V \mid V^{2+}$	$V^{2+} + 2e^- \rightleftharpoons V$	−1.18
$Zn \mid Zn^{2+}$	$Zn^{2+} + 2e^- \rightleftharpoons Zn$	−0.763
$Tl \mid Tl\,I \mid I^-$	$Tl\,I\,(s) + e^- \rightleftharpoons Tl + I^-$	−0.753
$Cr \mid Cr^{3+}$	$Cr^{3+} + 3e^- \rightleftharpoons Cr$	−0.744

(continued)

(continued)

STANDARD ELECTRODE POTENTIAL IN AQUEOUS SOLUTIONS AT 25°C		
Electrode	**Electrode Reaction**	**$E°_{red}(V)$**
$Tl \mid TlBr \mid Br^-$	$TlBr(s) + e^- \rightleftharpoons Tl + Br^-$	-0.658
$Pt \mid U^{3+}, U^{4+}$	$U^{4+} + e^- \rightleftharpoons U^{3+}$	-0.61
$Fe \mid Fe^{2+}$	$Fe^{2+} + 2e^- \rightleftharpoons Fe$	-0.440
$Cd \mid Cd^{2+}$	$Cd^{2+} + 2e^- \rightleftharpoons Cd$	-0.403
$Pb \mid PbSO_4 \mid SO_4^{2-}$	$PbSO_4 + 2e^- \rightleftharpoons Pb + SO_4^{2-}$	-0.359
$Tl \mid Tl^+$	$Tl^+ + e^- \rightleftharpoons Tl$	-0.3363
$Ag \mid AgI \mid I^-$	$Ag\,I + e^- \rightleftharpoons Ag + I^-$	0.152
$Pb \mid Pb^{2+}$	$Pb^{2+} + 2e^- \rightleftharpoons Pb$	-0.126
$Pt \mid D_2 \mid D^+$	$2D^+ + 2e^- \rightleftharpoons D_2$	-0.0034
$Pt \mid H_2 \mid H^+$	$2H^+ + 2e^- \rightleftharpoons H_2$	-0.0000
$Ag \mid AgBr \mid Br^-$	$AgBr + e^- \rightleftharpoons Ag + Br^-$	$+0.071$
$Ag \mid AgCl \mid Cl^-$	$AgCl + e^- \rightleftharpoons Ag + Cl^-$	$+0.2225$
$Pt \mid Hg \mid Hg_2Cl_2 \mid Cl^-$	$Hg_2Cl_2 + 2e^- \rightleftharpoons 2Cl^- + 2Hg(l)$	$+0.2676$
$Cu \mid Cu^{2+}$	$Cu^{2+} + 2e^- \rightleftharpoons Cu$	$+0.337$
$Pt \mid I_2 \mid I^-$	$I_2 + 2e^- \rightleftharpoons 2I^-$	$+0.536$
$Pt \mid O_2 \mid H_2O_2$	$O_2 + 2H^+ + 2e^- \rightleftharpoons H_2O_2$	$+0.682$
$Pt \mid Fe^{2+}, Fe^{3+}$	$Fe^{3+} + e^- \rightleftharpoons Fe^{2+}$	$+0.771$
$Ag \mid Ag^+$	$Ag^+ + e^- \rightleftharpoons Ag$	$+0.7991$
$Au \mid AuCl_4^-, Cl^-$	$AuCl_4^- + 3e^- \rightleftharpoons Au + 4Cl^-$	$+1.00$
$Pt \mid Br_2 \mid Br^-$	$Br_2 + 2e^- \rightleftharpoons 2Br^-$	$+1.065$
$Pt \mid Tl^+, Tl^{3+}$	$Tl^{3+} + 2e^- \rightleftharpoons Tl^+$	$+1.25$
$Pt \mid H^+, Cr_2O_7^{2-}, Cr^{3+}$	$Cr_2O_7^{2-} + 14H^+ + 6e^- \rightleftharpoons 2Cr^{3+} + 7H_2O$	$+1.33$
$Pt \mid Cl_2 \mid Cl^-$	$Cl_2 + 2e^- \rightleftharpoons 2Cl^-$	$+1.3595$
$Pt \mid Ce^{4+}, Ce^{3+}$	$Ce^{4+} + e^- \rightleftharpoons Ce^{3+}$	$+1.45$
$Au \mid Au^{3+}$	$Au^{3+} + 3e^- \rightleftharpoons Au$	$+1.50$
$Pt \mid Mn^{2+}, MnO_4^-$	$MnO_4^- + 8H^+ + 5e^- \rightleftharpoons Mn^{2+} + 4H_2O$	$+1.51$
$Au \mid Au^+$	$Au^+ + e^- \rightleftharpoons Au$	$+1.68$
$PbSO_4 \mid PbO_2 \mid H_2SO_4$	$PbO_2 + SO_4^{2-} + 4H^+ + 2e^- \rightleftharpoons PbSO_4 + 2H_2O$	$+1.685$
$Pt \mid F_2 \mid F^-$	$F_2(g) + 2e^- \rightleftharpoons 2F^-$	$+2.87$

(continued)

(continued)

STANDARD ELECTRODE POTENTIAL IN AQUEOUS SOLUTIONS AT 25°C		
Electrode	**Electrode Reaction**	**E°$_{red}$(V)**
Basic Solutions		
Pt | SO$_3^{2-}$, SO$_4^{2-}$	SO$_4^{2-}$ + H$_2$O + 2e$^-$ $\rightleftharpoons$ SO$_3^{2-}$ + 2OH$^-$	−0.93
Pt | H$_2$ | OH$^-$	2H$_2$O + 2e$^-$ $\rightleftharpoons$ H$_2$ + 2OH$^-$	−0.828
Ag | Ag(NH$_3$)$_2^+$, NH$_3$(aq)	Ag(NH$_3$)$_2^+$ + e$^-$ $\rightleftharpoons$ Ag + 2NH$_3$ (aq)	+0.373
Pt | O$_2$ | OH$^-$	O$_2$ + 2H$_2$O + 4e$^-$ $\rightleftharpoons$ 4OH$^-$	+0.401
Pt | MnO$_2$ | MnO$_4^-$	MnO$_4^-$ + 2H$_2$O + 3e$^-$ $\rightleftharpoons$ MnO$_2$ + 4OH$^-$	+0.588

    i. Half equations with negative electrode reduction potentials lose electrons most readily and tend to go in reverse. These species are best reducing agents.

    ii. Half equations with positive electrode reduction potentials gain electrons most readily and tend to go forward. These species are best oxidizing agents.

2. The standard electrode reduction potential of a half cell, E$^\theta$, is defined as the electrode potential of a half cell, measured relative to a standard hydrogen electrode, which has a value of 0.00V, measured under standard conditions.

    i. Standard conditions are 25°C (298K), any gases at a pressure of 1 atm, and all solutions at concentrations of 1M.

B. GALVANIC CELLS

1. A galvanic cell generates electrical energy from a spontaneous REDOX reaction. Connecting two half cells that have different electrode potentials forms an electrochemical cell (battery). For example, see the following diagram.

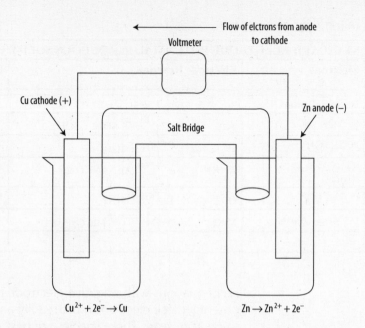

$$Cu^{2+} + 2e^- \rightarrow Cu \qquad\qquad Zn \rightarrow Zn^{2+} + 2e^-$$

2. A high-resistance voltmeter is used to measure the voltage.

3. A salt bridge connects the two half cells. It can be made from a piece of filter paper soaked in an inert ionic solution, often KCl or KNO_3. It allows the flow of ions.

4. The electrons flow through the wire, toward the more positive half cell where reduction takes place. This is the *cathode*.

5. The electrons flow through the wire, from the more negative half cell where oxidation takes place. This is the *anode*.

6. The voltage in the cell can be calculated using
$$E^\theta_{cell} = E^\theta_{reduced} - E^\theta_{oxidized.}$$

7. The relationship between Gibbs Free Energy and E^θ_{cell} is summarized by the expression $\Delta G^\theta = - n\,F\,E^\theta$, where F = Faraday constant = 96,500 J/V mol, and n = number of moles of electrons transferred.

8. The Nernst equation can be used to calculate the voltage in a cell when conditions are not standard. One form of the equation is $E_{cell} = E^\theta - \dfrac{RT}{nF}\,\ln Q$, where R = 8.314 J/K mol, T = Kelvin temperature, n = number of electrons transferred, F = Faraday constant, E^θ = the voltage generated *if* the conditions were standard, ln represents the natural logarithm, and Q = reaction quotient (see Chapter 29).

C. ELECTROLYTIC CELLS

1. *Electrolysis* is the process in which electrical energy is used to cause a nonspontaneous REDOX reaction to occur. Electrolysis occurs in an electrolytic cell and it is the opposite of a galvanic cell. See the following diagram.

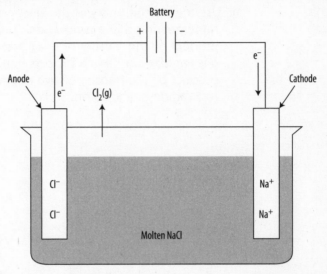

2. *Anions* in the electrolyte solution are attracted toward the anode, where they undergo oxidation. Electrons flow from the anode to the cathode, where cations undergo reduction.

3. The electrolysis of aqueous solutions can be more complicated because water is present that can ALSO undergo REDOX processes. See the following examples.

$$2H_2O_{(l)} \leftrightarrows O_{2(g)} + 4H^+_{(aq)} + 4e^-, \; E^\theta = -1.23 \text{ V}$$

$$2H_2O_{(l)} + 2e^- \leftrightarrows H_{2(g)} + 2OH^-_{(aq)}, \; E^\theta = -0.83 \text{ V}$$

When this is the case, decisions based upon SERP values must be made about the relative likelihood of one process over another.

4. The amount of a substance produced in an electrolytic cell can be calculated using Faraday's law. This quantitative aspect of electrolysis can be approached as follows.

    i. Calculate the number of Faradays passed by applying the following formula: $q = I \, t$, where I = current in Amps, q = charge in Coulombs, and t = time in s.

ii. Secondly, convert q to Faradays.

Number of Faradays =

Charge in coulombs (q) $\times \dfrac{1 \text{ Faraday}}{96,500 \text{ Coulombs}}$

iii. Use the stoichiometry of the electrode process, remembering that a process that produces a product by the transfer of *one* electron will require *one* Faraday, and that a process that produces a product by the transfer of *two* electrons will require *two* Faradays, and so on.

PRECIPITATION INCLUDING BASIC SOLUBILITY RULES

I. PRECIPITATION REACTIONS

A. PRINCIPLES AND SOLUBILITY RULES

1. Some ionic compounds are very soluble in water, while others are less so.

2. A precipitation reaction occurs when a *double displacement* (*double replacement*) reaction takes place between two aqueous solutions, and certain cation and anion combinations lead to the formation of an insoluble compound. The insoluble compound is called a *precipitate (ppt.)*.

3. The solubility rules allow predictions about which combinations of ions will form precipitates.

Solubility Rules

SOLUBLE	INSOLUBLE
Group 1 and ammonium	Hydroxides
Nitrates, hydrogen carbonates, chlorates, ethanoates, and perchlorates	(**EXCEPT** Group 1 and ammonium; hydroxides of Ca^{2+}, Sr^{2+}, and Ba^{2+} are slightly soluble)
Chlorides, bromides, and iodides (**EXCEPT** Pb^{2+}, Ag^+, and Hg_2^{2+})	Carbonates, phosphates, sulfites, chromates, and sulfides
Sulfates (**EXCEPT** Pb^{2+}, Ag^+, Hg_2^{2+}, Sr^{2+}, Ba^{2+}, and Ca^{2+})	(**EXCEPT** Group 1 and ammonium; sulfides of Group 2 are soluble)

Test Tip *You must commit these solubility rules to memory. They are a crucial piece of knowledge that you must carry with you into the test.*

B. FULL EQUATIONS, IONIC EQUATIONS, AND NET IONIC EQUATIONS—Consider the reaction between an aqueous solution of silver nitrate and an aqueous solution of sodium iodide.

1. *Full equation.* A double displacement reaction takes place. Solubility rules predict that the silver iodide is insoluble and therefore will form a precipitate. The same rules predict that sodium nitrate will remain in aqueous solution because it is soluble.

$$AgNO_{3(aq)} + NaI_{(aq)} \rightarrow AgI_{(s)} + NaNO_{3(aq)}$$

2. *Ionic equation.* An ionic equation shows all the aqueous ions fully ionized in solution, and any insoluble solids in a nonionized state.

$$Ag^+_{(aq)} + NO_3{}^-_{(aq)} + Na^+_{(aq)} + I^-_{(aq)} \rightarrow AgI_{(s)} + Na^+_{(aq)} + NO_3{}^-_{(aq)}$$

3. *Net ionic equation.* In the ionic equation, the sodium and nitrate ions are in the aqueous state on both sides of the equation and do not take part in the reaction because they remain unchanged. They are said to be "spectator ions" and they can be canceled out.

$$Ag^+_{(aq)} + \cancel{NO_3{}^-_{(aq)}} + \cancel{Na^+_{(aq)}} + I^-_{(aq)} \rightarrow AgI_{(s)} + \cancel{Na^+_{(aq)}} + \cancel{NO_3{}^-_{(aq)}}$$

This leaves an equation that shows only the ions that take part in the reaction. This is called the *net ionic equation.*

$$Ag^+_{(aq)} + I^-_{(aq)} \rightarrow AgI_{(s)}$$

C. IDENTIFICATION OF PRECIPITATES IN QUALITATIVE CHEMISTRY—The formation of colored precipitates is an important tool in aqueous qualitative chemistry. The following table summarizes a few of the more common reactions that are used in qualitative analysis.

Qualitative Tests for Some Anions and Cations

Test for ANIONS	Reagent Added	Expected Result	Notes
$SO_4{}^{2-}_{(aq)}$	$Ba^{2+}_{(aq)}$, often in the form of $BaCl_{2(aq)}$	White ppt. of $BaSO_{4(s)}$	
$Cl^-_{(aq)}$	$Ag^+_{(aq)}$, often in the form of $AgNO_{3(aq)}$	White ppt. of $AgCl_{(s)}$	ppt. soluble in dilute, $NH_{3(aq)}$

(*continued*)

Qualitative Tests for Some Anions and Cations (*continued*)

Test for ANIONS	Reagent Added	Expected Result	Notes
$Br^-_{(aq)}$	$Ag^+_{(aq)}$, often in the form of $AgNO_{3(aq)}$	Cream ppt. of $AgBr_{(s)}$	ppt. soluble in conc., $NH_{3(aq)}$
$I^-_{(aq)}$	$Ag^+_{(aq)}$, often in the form of $AgNO_{3(aq)}$	Pale yellow ppt. of $AgI_{(s)}$	ppt. insoluble in $NH_{3(aq)}$
$Ag^+_{(aq)}$	Aqueous halide ion ($Cl^-_{(aq)}$, $Br^-_{(aq)}$ $I^-_{(aq)}$)	ppt. of halide salt (see above)	
$Ba^{2+}_{(aq)}$	$SO_4^{2-}_{(aq)}$	White ppt. of $BaSO_{4(s)}$	
$Pb^{2+}_{(aq)}$	$I^-_{(aq)}$	Yellow ppt. of $PbI_{2(s)}$	Other halide ions will also precipitate Pb^{2+} with different colors
$Ni^{2+}_{(aq)}$	$OH^-_{(aq)}$, often in the form of $NaOH_{(aq)}$	Green ppt.	ppt. is gelatinous
$Al^{3+}_{(aq)}$	$OH^-_{(aq)}$, often in the form of $NaOH_{(aq)}$	White ppt.	ppt. dissolves in excess hydroxide
$Cu^{2+}_{(aq)}$	$OH^-_{(aq)}$, often in the form of $NaOH_{(aq)}$	Blue ppt.	
$Fe^{2+}_{(aq)}$	$OH^-_{(aq)}$, often in the form of $NaOH_{(aq)}$	Dirty green ppt.	
$Fe^{3+}_{(aq)}$	$OH^-_{(aq)}$, often in the form of $NaOH_{(aq)}$	Red/brown ppt.	
$Zn^{2+}_{(aq)}$	$OH^-_{(aq)}$, often in the form of $NaOH_{(aq)}$	White ppt.	ppt. dissolves in excess hydroxide

Test Tip

The recognition of some common colors can be a really useful tool in "unlocking" some questions on the test. Try to remember as many as possible.

PART V:

STOICHIOMETRY

MOLE CONCEPT, AVOGADRO'S NUMBER, AND MOLAR MASS

I. THE MOLE CONCEPT AND AVOGADRO'S NUMBER

A. AVOGADRO'S NUMBER AND THE MOLE

1. In chemistry, the amount of a substance is measured in moles (mols).

2. The mole is a standard number of particles (atoms, ions, molecules, or formula units) and is defined as the amount of any substance that contains the same number of particles, as there are C^{12} atoms in 12.00 g of the C^{12} isotope.

3. Just as "1 pair" means 2, "1 dozen" means 12, and "1 baker's dozen" means 13, "1 mole" means 6.02×10^{23}. This is known as *Avogadro's number*. For example, 1 mole of atoms = 6.02×10^{23} atoms.

Test Tip

The mole concept, use of Avogadro's number, and calculations associated with it are arguably the most important concept in all of chemistry. It is essential that you become familiar and comfortable with their use.

B. MASS NUMBERS

1. The mass numbers associated with each element on the periodic table have a specific meaning. They represent the mass, in grams, of 1 mole of atoms of that element.

2. For example, 16.00 g of oxygen atoms contains 1 mole of oxygen atoms, i.e., 6.02×10^{23} atoms of oxygen.

II. ATOMIC MASS, MOLECULAR MASS, AND FORMULA MASS

A. ATOMIC MASS

1. Relative atomic mass is defined as the weighted average of the masses of all the atoms in a normal isotopic sample of the element based upon the scale where 1 mole of atoms of the C^{12} isotope has a mass of exactly 12.00 g.

2. We have seen previously how elements occur in nature as a number of different isotopes and as a result they often have mass numbers that are averages and that are not integers.

3. The average relative atomic masses shown on the periodic table can be used to determine the relative masses of molecules and formula units by simple summation.

*While it is **not** necessary to learn the atomic masses for the elements (because you will have a periodic table in the test), if you can learn a few of the more common ones you will be able to do questions involving them without looking at the periodic table, and therefore be able to answer those questions more quickly. Some of the more common ones are H (1.0079, rounded to 1), C (12.011, rounded to 12), O (16.00, rounded to 16), N (14.007, rounded to 14), Cl (35.453, rounded to 35.5), and S (32.06, rounded to 32).*

B. MOLECULAR MASS

1. The molecular mass of a molecule is determined by the addition of the individual atomic masses.

2. Because covalently bonded compounds form molecules, the term *molecular mass* is usually reserved for those compounds.

C. FORMULA MASS

1. The formula mass of an ionic compound is determined by the addition of the individual atomic masses.

2. Because ionically bonded compounds do not form molecules, the term *molecular mass* is usually not used for those compounds, and the equivalent (but different) term, *formula mass* is used.

EMPIRICAL AND MOLECULAR FORMULA

I. PERCENTAGE BY MASS COMPOSITION

A. CALCULATION OF PERCENTAGE BY MASS COMPOSITION

1. To determine the percentage by mass composition of an individual element within a compound, simply express the mass of each element as a percentage of the total mass of the compound.

2. See the following example.

   i. A compound with the formula $C_2H_4O_2$ has a total mass of $(2)(12.011) + (4)(1.0079) + (2)(16.00) = 60.05$.

   ii. Percentages of each element, expressed as a function of the total mass, are shown as follows.

   Carbon $\dfrac{[(2)(12.011)]}{60.05} = 40.00\%$

   Hydrogen $\dfrac{[(4)(1.0079)]}{60.05} = 6.71\%$

   Oxygen $\dfrac{[(2)(16.00)]}{60.05} = 53.29\%$

II. EMPIRICAL FORMULA

A. DEFINITION

1. The empirical formula of a compound is the simplest whole-number (integer) ratio of the atoms of each element in that compound.

B. CALCULATION

1. Empirical formulae can be calculated from percentage by mass data.
2. See the following for the method for calculating empirical formula from percentage by mass data.
    i. Take the percentage of each element and assume a sample of 100 g. (This assumption converts percentages to masses.)
    ii. Convert the masses of each element to the moles of each element by dividing each element's mass by the corresponding atomic mass taken from the periodic table.
    iii. Find the ratio of the moles calculated in (ii) by dividing each of the moles by the smallest number of moles.
    iv. The results from (iii) will be in a convenient ratio and gives the empirical formula.

It may be that the ratio includes a decimal (fraction) such as 0.500, 0.333, 0.250, and so on. If so, then because empirical formulae are simplest, WHOLE-number ratios, you must multiply all of the numbers in the ratio by 2, 3, or 4 as appropriate in order to remove the decimal.

3. Following is an example of an empirical formula calculation. Calculate the empirical formula of a compound containing 40.1% carbon, 6.70% hydrogen, and 53.3% oxygen by mass.

Calculation of an Empirical Formula

	C	H	O
Percentage (%) (and by Assuming a 100 g Sample) Also the Mass in Grams	40.0	6.71	53.29
Molar Mass of the Element	12.011	1.0079	16.00

(continued)

Calculation of an Empirical Formula (*continued*)

	C	H	O
Moles = Mass in Grams ÷ Molar Mass	3.34	6.55	3.33
Divide by Smallest Number of Moles	$(3.34/3.33) = 1$	$(6.55/3.33) = 2$	$(3.33/3.33) = 1$
Ratio is the Empirical Formula		$C_1H_2O_1$ or CH_2O	

When performing empirical formula calculations, avoid rounding up or down too much in the middle of the calculation, and be lenient with significant figures.

III. MOLECULAR FORMULA

A. GENERAL PRINCIPLE

1. Unlike the empirical formula (which shows the *simplest* whole-number ratio), the molecular formula of a compound shows the *exact* whole-number ratio of the different elements in a compound.

2. Like the empirical formula, the numbers of each element are recorded using a subscript to the right of the element's symbol. When only 1 atom is present, the subscript 1 is assumed (understood), and not written.

B. THE FOLLOWING DESCRIBES THE RELATIONSHIP BETWEEN THE MOLECULAR FORMULA AND THE EMPIRICAL FORMULA

1. The molecular formula will be some simple, integer multiple of the empirical formula. For example, a compound with an empirical formula of CH_2O will have a molecular formula of either CH_2O, or $C_2H_4O_2$, or $C_3H_6O_3$ and so on, where the empirical formula is multiplied by either, 1, or 2, or 3, and so on.

2. To establish the correct multiplier, and therefore find the molecular formula, it is necessary to know the molecular mass of the compound.

    i. In the preceding example, given a molecular mass of 60, divide the molecular mass of the compound by the mass of the empirical formula. In this case, the mass of the empirical formula, CH_2O is as follows.

$$12.0011 + (2)(1.0079) + 16.00 = 30.03$$

$$\frac{\text{molar mass}}{\text{mass of empirical formula}} = \frac{60.0}{30.0} = 2$$

    ii. The answer to i. is the multiplier, so $(2)(CH_2O) = C_2H_4O_2$ is the molecular formula.

CHEMICAL EQUATIONS AND **BALANCING** CHEMICAL EQUATIONS

I. **CHEMICAL EQUATIONS**—Chemical equations are a shorthand method used to illustrate and summarize what happens during a chemical reaction.

A. THE BASIC ANATOMY OF A CHEMICAL EQUATION

1. The formulae of reactants are written to the left of the arrow.
2. The formulae of the products are written to the right of the arrow.
3. Stoichiometric numbers in front of each reactant and product show the molar ratio of reactants and products.

B. WRITING AN EQUATION—There are a number of steps to writing a chemical equation.

1. Write the equation in words (this may or may not be required).
2. Replace the words with correct formulae for all the substances.
3. Add state symbols as subscripts (this may or may not be required).

   (s) for solid, (l) for liquid, (g) for gas, (aq) for aqueous (meaning in solution with water)

II. **BALANCING CHEMICAL EQUATIONS**

A. CONSERVATION OF MASS

1. Once the equation has been written, it must be balanced because it is not possible to create or destroy matter.

2. All atoms that exist at the start of a reaction must also exist (and be accounted for) at the end of the reaction.

B. METHOD OF BALANCING

1. Balance each element in turn, remembering to multiply any brackets out carefully. This process is essentially one of trial and error, but the following tips can help.

   i. If any element appears in only one compound on each side of the equation, try balancing that first.

   ii. Any elements that appear in more than one compound should be balanced last.

   iii. If one of the reactants or products appears as the free element, try balancing that last.

2. When balancing, only place numbers in front of whole formulae. Do not change the (correct) formulae of any of the reactants or products, or add any extra formulae.

Test Tip

If you are having difficulty in balancing an equation, go back and carefully check all of the formulae. If mistakes are made in constructing formulae, this can sometimes make an equation impossible to balance.

3. For example, balance the equation that summarizes the reaction between sulfuric acid and potassium hydrogen carbonate, to produce potassium sulfate, water, and carbon dioxide.

   i. Write the equation and assess atoms initially present.

$$H_2SO_4 + KHCO_3 \rightarrow K_2SO_4 + H_2O + CO_2$$

Left-hand side	Right-hand side
3 H	2 H
1 S	1 S
7 O	7 O
1 K	2 K
1 C	1 C

   ii. Work from left to right, as shown in the following section.

   a) H appears in more than one compound, so leave until later.

b) S is balanced.

c) O is balanced.

d) There is insufficient K on the left, so change the 1 in front of $KHCO_3$ to a 2, to give the following equation.

$$H_2SO_4 + 2KHCO_3 \rightarrow K_2SO_4 + H_2O + CO_2$$

Left-hand side	Right-hand side
4 H	2 H
1 S	1 S
10 O	7 O
2 K	2 K
2 C	1 C

iii. Now the C and O are unbalanced. Change the 1 in front of CO_2 to a 2, as shown in the following equation.

$$H_2SO_4 + 2KHCO_3 \rightarrow K_2SO_4 + H_2O + 2CO_2$$

Left-hand side	Right-hand side
4 H	2 H
1 S	1 S
10 O	9 O
2 K	2 K
2 C	2 C

iv. Finally, address the H and O. By simply changing the 1 in front of the H_2O to a 2, both are balanced.

$$H_2SO_4 + 2KHCO_3 \rightarrow K_2SO_4 + 2H_2O + 2CO_2$$

Left-hand side	Right-hand side
4 H	4 H
1 S	1 S
10 O	10 O
2 K	2 K
2 C	2 C

When counting the number of atoms present, take care to multiply out brackets carefully, and to apply stoichiometric numbers carefully. For example, in the following reaction, the subscript 3 that follows the nitrate ion (NO_3^-) in $Al(NO_3)_3$ applies only to the N atoms and the O atoms to give a total of 1 Al, but 3 Ns and 9 Os in $Al(NO_3)_3$. However, the stoichiometric number 3 in front of HNO_3 means all atoms within HNO_3 must be multiplied by 3 to give a total of 3 Hs, 3 Ns, and 9 Os in $3HNO_3$.

$$Al(OH)_3 + 3HNO_3 \rightarrow Al(NO_3)_3 + 3H_2O$$

STOICHIOMETRY CALCULATIONS

I. **PRINCIPLES OF CALCULATIONS FROM BALANCED EQUATIONS**—The stoichiometric numbers in a balanced equation give the reacting ratios of the moles of products and reactants.

A. GENERAL METHOD

1. Convert any given data to moles. This is necessary because the balanced chemical equation gives the ratio of *moles* and not the ratio of masses, volumes, or concentrations.
2. Find the number of moles of other substances by applying the molar ratio from the stoichiometric numbers in the balanced chemical equation.
3. If necessary (depending on the question), convert the moles of the new substance back to mass, volume, or concentration.

> *Using dimensional analysis (factor label method) is not entirely necessary because the questions on the SAT subject test are all multiple choice and there is no need to show your work. However, it is a really useful way to organize your thoughts and can help you avoid silly errors.*

II. **EXAMPLES OF CALCULATIONS FROM BALANCED EQUATIONS**

A. THOSE WHERE MASSES ARE INITIALLY GIVEN

1. These problems involve converting masses of solids, liquids, or gases to moles by applying the following formula.

$$\text{moles} = \frac{\text{mass}}{\text{molar mass}}$$

2. For example, consider the combustion of methane gas (CH_4) in oxygen gas to produce carbon dioxide gas and water.

$$CH_4 + 2O_2 \rightarrow CO_2 + 2H_2O$$

3. Answer the following question: calculate the mass of O_2 required, in order to produce 4.40 g of carbon dioxide.

   i. Convert the mass of carbon dioxide to moles of carbon dioxide.

$$\frac{4.40 \text{ g of } CO_2}{} \quad \frac{1 \text{ mole of } CO_2}{44.0 \text{ g of } CO_2}$$

   ii. Apply the ratio from the balanced equation to find moles of oxygen.

$$\frac{4.40 \text{ g of } CO_2}{} \quad \frac{1 \text{ mole of } CO_2}{44.0 \text{ g of } CO_2} \quad \frac{2 \text{ moles of } O_2}{1 \text{ mole of } CO_2}$$

   iii. Convert moles of oxygen to mass of oxygen.

$$\frac{4.40 \text{ g of } CO_2}{} \quad \frac{1 \text{ mole of } CO_2}{44.0 \text{ g of } CO_2} \quad \frac{2 \text{ moles of } O_2}{1 \text{ mole of } CO_2} \quad \frac{32.0 \text{ g of } O_2}{1 \text{ mole of } O_2}$$

   iv. Do the math and cancel units.

$$\frac{4.40 \text{ g of } CO_2}{} \quad \frac{1 \text{ mole of } CO_2}{44.0 \text{ g of } CO_2} \quad \frac{2 \text{ moles of } O_2}{1 \text{ mole of } CO_2} \quad \frac{32.0 \text{ g of } O_2}{1 \text{ mole of } O_2}$$

$$= 6.40 \text{ g of } O_2$$

B. THOSE WHERE CONCENTRATIONS AND VOLUMES OF SOLUTIONS ARE INITIALLY GIVEN

1. These problems involve converting volumes and concentrations of solutions to moles by applying the following formula.

moles = concentration   volume

2. For example, consider the reaction of hydrochloric acid with sodium hydroxide to produce sodium chloride and water.

$$HCl + NaOH \rightarrow NaCl + H_2O$$

3. Answer the following question: calculate the volume of 0.100 M NaOH required to react with 25.0 mL of 0.125 M HCl.

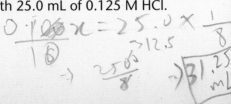

i. Convert volume and concentration of HCl to moles of HCl.

$$\frac{0.125 \text{ moles of HCl}}{1.0 \text{ L}} \quad \frac{1.0 \text{ L}}{1000 \text{ mL}} \quad 25.0 \text{ mL}$$

ii. Apply the ratio from the balanced equation to find moles of NaOH.

$$\frac{0.125 \text{ moles of HCl}}{1.0 \text{ L}} \quad \frac{1.0 \text{ L}}{1000 \text{ mL}} \quad 25.0 \text{ mL} \quad \frac{1 \text{ mole of NaOH}}{1 \text{ mole of HCl}}$$

iii. Convert moles of NaOH to volume of NaOH.

$$\frac{0.125 \text{ moles of HCl}}{1.0 \text{ L}} \quad \frac{1.0 \text{ L}}{1000 \text{ mL}} \quad 25.0 \text{ mL} \quad \frac{1 \text{ mole of NaOH}}{1 \text{ mole of HCl}} \quad \frac{1.0 \text{ L}}{0.100 \text{ mols of NaOH}}$$

iv. Do the math and cancel the units.

$$\frac{0.125 \text{ moles of HCl}}{1.0 \text{ L}} \quad \frac{1.0 \text{ L}}{1000 \text{ mL}} \quad 25.0 \text{ mL} \quad \frac{1 \text{ mole of NaOH}}{1 \text{ mole of HCl}} \quad \frac{1.0 \text{ L}}{0.100 \text{ moles of NaOH}}$$

$$= 0.03125 \text{ L of NaOH}$$

C. THOSE WHERE VOLUMES OF GASES (AT STP) ARE INITIALLY GIVEN

1. These problems involve converting volumes of gases to moles by applying the following relationship.

   1 mole of any gas at STP occupies a volume of 22.4 L

Test Tip

The conversion factor of 1.00 mole of gas is equivalent to a volume of 22.4 L is only applicable under conditions of standard temperature and pressure, STP. Those conditions are 273.15 K and 1.00 atm.

2. For example, consider the combustion of methane gas (CH_4) in oxygen gas to produce carbon dioxide gas and water.

$$CH_4 + 2O_2 \rightarrow CO_2 + 2H_2O$$

36

3. Calculate the volume of carbon dioxide gas produced at STP, when starting with 36.0 L of methane at STP.

    i. Convert the volume of methane to moles of methane.

$$\dfrac{36.0 \text{ L of } CH_4}{} \quad \dfrac{1 \text{ mole of } CH_4}{22.4 \text{ L of } CH_4}$$

    ii. Apply the ratio from the balanced equation to find moles of carbon dioxide.

$$\dfrac{36.0 \text{ L of } CH_4}{} \quad \dfrac{1 \text{ mole of } CH_4}{22.4 \text{ L of } CH_4} \quad \dfrac{1 \text{ mole of } CO_2}{1 \text{ mole of } CH_4}$$

    iii. Convert moles of carbon dioxide to the volume of carbon dioxide.

$$\dfrac{36.0 \text{ L of } CH_4}{} \quad \dfrac{1 \text{ mole of } CH_4}{22.4 \text{ L of } CH_4} \quad \dfrac{1 \text{ mole of } CO_2}{1 \text{ mole of } CH_4} \quad \dfrac{22.4 \text{ L of } CO_2}{1 \text{ mole of } CO_2}$$

    iv. Do the math and cancel units.

$$\dfrac{36.0 \text{ L of } CH_4}{} \quad \dfrac{1 \text{ mole of } CH_4}{22.4 \text{ L of } CH_4} \quad \dfrac{1 \text{ mole of } CO_2}{1 \text{ mole of } CH_4} \quad \dfrac{22.4 \text{ L of } CO_2}{1 \text{ mole of } CO_2}$$

$$= 36.0 \text{ L of } CO_2$$

PERCENT YIELD AND LIMITING REACTANTS

I. LIMITING REACTANT

A. STOICHIOMETRIC PROPORTIONS

1. When all of the reactants in a chemical reaction are completely consumed, i.e., they are all converted to products, then the reactants are said to be in *stoichiometric proportions.*

    For example, in the following reaction, as long as the number of moles of oxygen is exactly double the number of moles of methane, then all of the reactants will be consumed during the reaction because the reactants are in the correct 1:2 stoichiometric ratio.

$$CH_4 + 2O_2 \rightarrow CO_2 + 2H_2O$$

2. In many real-world situations, the reactants in a chemical reaction do not come together in the perfect, stoichiometric proportions, and as a result one reactant is completely consumed, while others will be left over at the conclusion of the reaction.

B. EXCESS AND LIMITING REACTANT

1. *Limiting reactant.* When a single reactant is completely consumed during a reaction, and at the same time other reactants remain unreacted, the reactant that is completely consumed is said to be limiting, and is known as the *limiting reactant.*

2. Any reactants that are left unreacted after the limiting reactant has been consumed are said to be "in excess," and are known as *excess reactants.*

3. The *limiting reactant* is named as such because it limits the amount of product that can be formed because it "runs out" and hence the reaction stops, even though other reactants may still be available for reaction.

4. There are three methods commonly employed to find the limiting reactant. Consider the following data, which is applied to all three methods that follow.

   80.00 g of methane are brought together with 100.0 g of O_2 in the reaction summarized in the following equation. Find the limiting reactant.

$$CH_4 + 2O_2 \rightarrow CO_2 + 2H_2O$$

Because all three methods require masses to be converted to moles (because we will be using molar ratios for comparison), that is the first step. These mole amounts will be used in all three methods that follow.

$$\text{moles of } CH_4 = \frac{80.00 \text{ g of } CH_4}{} \frac{1 \text{ mole of } CH_4}{16.03 \text{ g of } CH_4}$$

$$= 4.99 \text{ moles of } CH_4$$

$$\text{moles of } O_2 = \frac{100.00 \text{ g of } O_2}{} \frac{1 \text{ mole of } O_2}{32.00 \text{ g of } O_2}$$

$$= 3.125 \text{ moles of } O_2$$

i. The first method is to compare the required reactant amounts to the actual reactant amounts.

   a) According to the following calculation, 4.99 moles of methane would require 9.98 moles of oxygen.

$$\frac{4.99 \text{ moles of } CH_4}{} \frac{2 \text{ moles of } O_2}{1 \text{ mole of } CH_4} = 9.98 \text{ moles of } O_2$$

   Because there are only 3.125 moles of oxygen in the original reaction mixture, there is insufficient oxygen to react with 4.99 moles of methane and therefore the oxygen in the limiting reactant.

   Following is an alternate calculation.

   b) According to the following calculation, 3.125 moles of oxygen would require 1.56 moles of methane.

$$\frac{3.125 \text{ moles of } O_2}{} \frac{1 \text{ mole of } CH_4}{2 \text{ moles of } O_2} = 1.56 \text{ moles of } CH_4$$

Because there are 4.99 moles of methane in the original reaction mixture, there is more than enough methane to react with 3.125 moles of oxygen and therefore the methane is the excess reactant.

ii. The second method is to compare product amounts.

   a) According to the following calculation, 4.99 moles of methane would produce 9.98 moles of water.

$$\frac{4.99 \text{ moles of } CH_4}{} \quad \frac{2 \text{ moles of } H_2O}{1 \text{ mole of } CH_4} = 9.98 \text{ moles of } H_2O$$

   b) According to the following calculation, 3.125 moles of oxygen would produce 3.125 moles of water.

$$\frac{3.125 \text{ moles of } O_2}{} \quad \frac{2 \text{ moles of } H_2O}{2 \text{ moles of } O_2} = 3.125 \text{ moles of } H_2O$$

Because oxygen produces the smaller amount of product, it is the limiting reactant.

iii. The third method is the stoichiometric number method. This is a short-cut method that involves dividing both of the initial molar amounts by the stoichiometric numbers associated with each reactant in the original equation.

for methane, $\dfrac{4.99}{1} = 4.99$, for oxygen, $\dfrac{3.125}{2} = 1.56$

In this case, the smallest number will reveal the limiting reactant, so again oxygen is found to be limiting.

C. SIGNIFICANCE OF LIMITING REACTANT

1. In any stoichiometric calculation that presents data for more than one reactant, it is essential to find the limiting reactant because the limiting reactant drives all other amounts.

Test Tip

Whenever a question gives data about more than one reactant that can be converted to moles, you must check for the limiting reactant.

2. Once the number of moles of the limiting reactant has been found, all stoichiometric ratios should be applied to IT, in order to calculate product or excess reactant quantities.

3. For example, using the same data as in section B4, calculate the following. In each case, use the limiting reactant previously established as the basis of the calculation.

    i. Calculate the moles of methane remaining in excess. 3.125 moles of oxygen will react with 1.56 moles of methane according to the following calculation.

$$\frac{3.125 \text{ moles of O}_2}{} \cdot \frac{1 \text{ mole of CH}_4}{2 \text{ moles of O}_2} = 1.56 \text{ moles of CH}_4$$

That is, $4.99 - 1.56$ moles of methane = 3.43 moles of methane remain in excess.

    ii. Calculate the moles of water formed in the reaction.

$$\frac{3.125 \text{ moles of O}_2}{} \cdot \frac{2 \text{ moles of H}_2\text{O}}{2 \text{ moles of O}_2} = 3.125 \text{ moles of H}_2\text{O}$$

II. PERCENTAGE YIELD

A. EFFICIENCY OF CHEMICAL REACTIONS

1. For a number of different reasons (not discussed here), in all chemical reactions, the actual yield of the products will be less than the yield calculated in theory.

2. Following is an example of a calculation of percentage (%) yield.

$$\% \text{ yield} = \frac{\text{actual yield of product}}{\text{theoretical yield}} \times 100$$

Actual and theoretical yields may be expressed in terms of mass or moles, but the units must be the same for each.

3. In the preceding example, we predict that 3.125 moles of water will be produced. If, in reality (i.e., when the experiment is carried out in the lab), we find only 2.000 moles of water are produced, then the percentage yield is as follows.

$$\% \text{ yield} = \frac{2.000}{3.125} \times 100 = 64.00\%$$

Test Tip

A calculated percentage yield of greater than 100% means that you have made a mistake somewhere. Go back and check your work!

PART VI:

EQUILIBRIUM AND REACTION RATES

EQUILIBRIUM AND EQUILIBRIUM CONSTANTS

 DYNAMIC EQUILIBRIUM AND EQUILIBRIUM CONSTANTS

A. ESTABLISHING A DYNAMIC EQUILIBRIUM

1. A dynamic equilibrium is established when, in a reversible reaction, the rate of the forward reaction is equal to the rate of the backward reaction.
2. Because the reactants are used up equally as fast as the products are produced, the concentrations of each substance are constant.

 *All concentrations being constant (not changing) is not the same thing as concentrations being equal (all having the same value). This is a common misconception and one that you must not have.*

B. A GENERIC EQUILIBRIUM CONSTANT

1. All equilibrium constants show the ratio of products to reactants present in an equilibrium mixture.
2. Depending on the reaction, one of three equilibrium constants may be calculated—Kc, Kp, or Ksp (also see Ka, Kb, and Kw in Chapter 19). In each case, the K expression has the following characteristics:
    i. Some aspects of the products are multiplied together in the numerator.

ii. Some aspects of the reactants are multiplied together in the denominator.

iii. All aspects of products and reactants are raised to the powers of the stoichiometric numbers found in the balanced chemical equation.

iv. It has a numerical value that is constant at constant temperature.

v. It does not include any values for pure solids or pure liquids.

C. SPECIFIC EQUILIBRIUM CONSTANTS

1. *Kc—using equilibrium concentrations.* Consider the following equilibrium where a, b, c, and d are the stoichiometric coefficients of substances A, B, C, and D, respectively.

$$aA_{(aq)} + bB_{(aq)} \rightleftarrows cC_{(aq)} + dD_{(aq)}$$

$$Kc = \frac{C^c \; D^d}{A^a \; B^b}, \text{ where [ ] represents concentration.}$$

2. *Kp—using equilibrium partial pressures, i.e., in gaseous equilibria.* Consider the following equilibrium where a, b, c, and d are the stoichiometric coefficients of substances A, B, C, and D, respectively.

$$aA_{(g)} + bB_{(g)} \rightleftarrows cC_{(g)} + dD_{(g)}$$

$$Kp = \frac{(ppC)^c \; (ppD)^d}{(ppA)^a \; (ppB)^b}, \text{ where pp represents partial pressure.}$$

3. *Ksp—using equilibrium concentrations in the specific case of sparingly soluble solids.* Consider the following equilibrium that is set up when a sparingly soluble solid is placed into water and an equilibrium is set up between the undissolved solid and its aqueous ions.

$$A_aB_{b\,(s)} \rightleftarrows aA^{b+}{}_{(aq)} + bB^{a-}{}_{(aq)}$$

An expression for Ksp can be written as follows:

$Ksp = [A^{b+}]^a \; [B^{a-}]^b$, where [ ] represents concentration.

II. K IN CALCULATIONS

A. Kc CALCULATIONS WHERE EQUILIBRIUM HAS ALREADY BEEN ESTABLISHED

1. Consider the following gaseous phase reaction, where gaseous butanoic acid ($C_3H_7CO_2H_{(g)}$) reacts with gaseous ethanol ($C_2H_5OH_{(g)}$) to produce the gaseous ester, ethyl butanoate ($C_3H_7CO_2C_2H_{5(g)}$), and steam, $H_2O_{(g)}$.

$$C_3H_7CO_2H_{(g)} + C_2H_5OH_{(g)} \rightleftarrows C_3H_7CO_2C_2H_{5(g)} + H_2O_{(g)}$$

Equilibrium was achieved and then the following data were collected. Moles of butanoic acid = 10.0, moles of ethanol = 10.0, moles of ethyl butanoate = 20.0, and moles of steam = 20.0. Calculate the equilibrium constant Kc, at this temperature.

   Because the equilibrium has been established, the moles of each substance can be converted to concentrations and go straight into the K expression. V is the volume and conveniently it cancels (if it did not cancel we would have to know its value). Each component of the mixture is raised to the stoichiometric number in the chemical equation.

$$Kc = \frac{\dfrac{20}{V}^{1} \ \dfrac{20}{V}^{1}}{\dfrac{10}{V}^{1} \ \dfrac{10}{V}^{1}} = 4$$

B. Kc CALCULATIONS WHERE INITIAL AMOUNTS ARE KNOWN BEFORE EQUILIBRIUM IS ESTABLISHED—THE USE OF ICE TABLES

1. Using the same reaction and the same Kc calculated in A. earlier (i.e., same reaction at the same temperature), calculate the number of moles of each substance present at equilibrium, when 1.00 mole of gaseous butanoic acid and 2.00 moles of gaseous ethanol are mixed.

   Set up an ICE table to find the moles of each substance present at equilibrium.

ICE Table

	$C_3H_7CO_2H_{(g)}$ + $C_2H_5OH_{(g)}$ $\rightleftarrows$ $C_3H_7CO_2C_2H_{5(g)}$ + $H_2O_{(g)}$			
Initial	1.00	2.00	0	0
Change	$-x$	$-x$	$+x$	$+x$
Equilibrium	$1.00 - x$	$2.00 - x$	$0 + x$	$0 + x$

Because this is same reaction as in A at the same temperature, we can use the same value for K.

$$Kc = \frac{\dfrac{x}{V}^1 \dfrac{x}{V}^1}{\dfrac{1.00-x}{V}^1 \dfrac{2.00-x}{V}^1} = 4$$

Again, volumes cancel and this leads to a quadratic equation and a value for x = 0.845.

Test Tip

It is not at all likely that you would be asked to solve a quadratic on the test; however, you should understand the chemistry of the preceding example, even if you ignore the math.

C. THE USE OF Kp IN CALCULATIONS

1. Dinitrogen tetroxide dissociates into nitrogen dioxide according to the following equation.

$$N_2O_{4(g)} \rightleftarrows 2NO_{2(g)}$$

When 1 mole of N_2O_4, at an equilibrium pressure of 3.0 atm, is 50.% dissociated, what is the value of Kp?

Set up an ICE table to find the moles of each substance present at equilibrium.

ICE Table

	$N_2O_{4(g)} \rightleftarrows 2NO_{2(g)}$	
Initial	1.0	0
Change	$-x$	$+2x$
Equilibrium	$1.0 - x$	$0 + 2x$

If we know the gas is 50.% dissociated, then half of it will be converted to NO_2 and $x = 0.5$. Converting to mole fractions, we find mole fraction of $N_2O_4 = \dfrac{0.5}{0.5 + 1.0} = 0.333$, mole fraction of $NO_2 = \dfrac{1.0}{0.5 + 1.0} = 0.666$. Then, partial pressure of $N_2O_4 = (0.333)(3.0 \text{ atm}) = 1.0 \text{ atm}$ and partial pressure of $NO_2 = (0.666)(3.0 \text{ atm}) = 2.00 \text{ atm}$.

$$Kp = \frac{2^2}{(1)^1} = 4$$

D. THE USE OF Ksp IN CALCULATIONS

1. Given that Ksp for $Ag_2SO_4 = 1.41 \times 10^{-5}$, calculate the molar solubility of Ag_2SO_4. The dissociation of Ag_2SO_4 in water is summarized in the following equation.

$$Ag_2SO_{4(s)} \rightleftarrows 2Ag^+_{(aq)} + SO_4^{2-}_{(aq)}$$

Because Ag_2SO_4 is a solid, it is omitted from the Ksp expression to give $Ksp = \left[Ag^+\right]^2 \left[SO_4^{2-}\right]$.

Set up an ICE table to find the moles of each substance present at equilibrium.

ICE Table

	$Ag_2SO_{4(s)} \rightleftarrows 2Ag^+_{(aq)} + SO_4^{2-}_{(aq)}$		
Initial	X	0	0
Change	$X - s$	$+2s$	$+s$
Equilibrium	$X - s$	$0 + 2s$	$0 + s$

$$Ksp = (2s)^2(s) = 4s^3 = 1.41 \times 10^{-5}$$

$$s = 0.0152 \text{ M}$$

III. THE RELATIONSHIP BETWEEN Kc AND Kp

A. HOMOGENEOUS, GASEOUS EQUILIBRIA

1. When a homogeneous gaseous equilibria is established, it is possible to express the equilibrium constant for the reaction in terms of concentration (Kc) or in terms of pressure (Kp).

    i. The relationship is summarized by the equation $Kp = Kc(RT)^{\Delta n}$, where Δn = (sum of the stoichiometric numbers of gaseous products − sum of the stoichiometric numbers gaseous reactants), T = temperature in K, and R = 0.0821 atm L K^{-1} mol^{-1}.

Test Tip

When n = 0—i.e., the sums of the stoichiometric numbers of the gases on each side of the equation are the same—then $(RT)^{\Delta n} = 1$, and Kp = Kc.

IV. RELATIONSHIP BETWEEN EQUILIBRIUM CONSTANT WHEN EQUATIONS ARE REARRANGED

A. CONSIDER THE REACTION, $N_2O_{4(g)} \rightleftarrows 2NO_{2(g)}$

1. The Kc expression is $K = \dfrac{[NO_2]^2}{[N_2O_4]}$.

2. If the chemical equation in (1) is reversed,

    $2NO_{2(g)} \rightleftarrows N_2O_{4(g)}$, the new Kc expression is $K = \dfrac{[N_2O_4]}{[NO_2]^2}$, which is the reciprocal of the K expression in (1).

3. If the chemical equation in (1) is halved, $\dfrac{1}{2}N_2O_{4(g)} \rightleftarrows NO_{2(g)}$, the new Kc expression is $K = \dfrac{[NO_2]}{[N_2O_4]^{\frac{1}{2}}}$, which is the square root of the K expression in (1).

4. If the chemical equation in (1) is doubled, $2N_2O_{4(g)} \rightleftarrows 4NO_{2(g)}$, the new Kc expression is $K = \dfrac{[NO_2]^4}{[N_2O_4]^2}$, which is the square of the K expression in (1).

V. REACTION QUOTIENT, Q

A. PRINCIPLE

1. *Format of Q.* The format of Q is exactly the same as the format of any given K, but the difference is that K is used when equilibrium has been established, and Q is used at any other (nonequilibrium) point.

B. USING Q TO MAKE PREDICTIONS ABOUT THE PROCEDURE OF AN EQUILIBRIUM REACTION

1. A calculated value of Q can be used to determine which way a reaction will proceed at any given point.
   i. if $Q > K$, then too many products are currently present and the reaction must proceed backwards (toward the reactants) to achieve equilibrium.
   ii. If $Q < K$, then insufficient products are currently present and the reaction must proceed forward (toward the products) to achieve equilibrium.
   iii. If $Q = K$, then equilibrium has been established and no shift is required.
2. See the following examples.
   i. This section shows how to use Q to predict the procedure of an equilibrium reaction.
   Consider the reaction, $N_{2(g)} + 3H_{2(g)} \rightleftarrows 2NH_{3(g)}$. At a certain temperature, the reaction has a value of $K = 24.0$. If N_2 at a pressure of 0.20 atm, H_2 at a pressure of 0.40 atm, and NH_3 at a pressure of 2.00 atm are brought together, in which direction will the reaction proceed?

   $$Q = \frac{2.00^2}{0.20^3 \ 0.40} = 1250$$

   Because $Q > K$, then too many products are present under these conditions and the reaction must proceed in the reverse direction in order to reach equilibrium.
   ii. This section shows how to use Q to predict the formation of precipitates.

If 750. mL of 0.010 M $BaCl_2$ and 150. mL of 0.010 M K_2SO_4 are mixed, will a precipitate form? (Ksp for barium sulfate = 1.1×10^{-10}.)

a) Calculate the moles of the ions that *may* form the precipitate by multiplying concentration by volume.

$$\text{Moles of } Ba^{2+} = (0.010)\,(0.750) = 0.00750 \text{ mols}$$

$$\text{Moles of } SO_4^{2-} = (0.010)\,(0.150) = 0.00150 \text{ mols}$$

b) Calculate the concentrations of these ions by remembering that when the solutions are mixed, the total volume = 750. mL + 150. mL = 900. mL = 0.900 L.

$$\text{Concentration of } Ba^{2+} \text{ after mixing} = \frac{0.00750}{0.900}$$
$$= 0.00833 \text{ M}$$

$$\text{Concentration of } SO_4{}^{2-} \text{ after mixing} = \frac{0.00150}{0.900}$$
$$= 0.00167 \text{ M}$$

c) Calculate Q, knowing the dissociation of $BaSO_4$ in water is summarized by $BaSO_{4(s)} \rightleftarrows Ba^{2+}{}_{(aq)} + SO_4^{2-}{}_{(aq)}$ and because $BaSO_4$ is a solid, it is omitted from the Ksp expression to give the following equation.

$$Ksp = Ba^{2+}\ SO_4^{2-}$$

and

$$Q = Ba^{2+}\ SO_4^{2-} = 0.00833\ \ 0.00167$$
$$= 1.39 \times 10^{-5}$$

Because Q > K, then too many products are present under these conditions and the reaction must proceed in the reverse direction in order to reach equilibrium. Because the solid is on the left-hand side of the equation when the reaction proceeds in the reverse direction, it will cause the precipitate to form.

VI. **THE COMMON ION EFFECT**

A. WHAT IS IT?

1. Attempting to dissolve a sparingly soluble, solid salt in pure water will yield different results than when attempting to dissolve the salt in a solvent that is not pure water.

2. When the solvent already contains some ions that are common to the solid salt, the *common ion effect* is observed.

B. WHAT IS ITS EFFECT?

1. Here's an example to illustrate its effect: silver chloride will dissolve more readily in pure water than it will in a solution that already contains either silver or chloride ions.

2. If there are already silver or chloride ions present, the following reaction will be shifted to the reactant side (see Le Chatelier's principle in Chapter 30), the solid will form more readily, and less will dissolve.

$$AgCl_{(s)} \rightleftarrows Ag^+_{(aq)} + Cl^-_{(aq)}$$

LE CHATELIER'S PRINCIPLE

I. LE CHATELIER'S PRINCIPLE

A. DEFINITION

1. Le Chatelier's principle states that in any equilibrium system, when a change is made to some factor such as temperature, pressure, or concentration, then the equilibrium shifts to counteract the imposed change. In other words, the equilibrium shifts to *oppose* the change.

To make predictions about shifts in equilibrium associated with temperature changes, you must understand the terms endothermic *and* exothermic. *An* endothermic *reaction is one that needs heat to make it go forward, and as such heat can be thought of as a "reactant." Endothermic reactions have positive ΔH values. An* exothermic *reaction is one where heat is produced when the reaction goes forward, so heat can be thought of as a "product." Exothermic reactions have negative ΔH values.*

Using these simplified ideas about heat being a "reactant" or a "product," it becomes easier to predict shifts in equilibrium based on temperature changes.

B. CONSIDER TWO EXAMPLES

1. The first example is the manufacture of ammonia (Haber process).

$$N_{2(g)} + 3H_{2(g)} \rightleftarrows 2NH_{3(g)}$$

ΔH = −92 kJ mol^{-1} (i.e., exothermic, where heat is a "product")

Remembering that the equilibrium will shift to oppose any change (i.e., it will do the *opposite* of the imposed change), we can predict the changes in equilibrium position when changes are made.

Summary of Changes in Equilibrium Position When Conditions Are Changed in the Haber Process

Change in External Factor	Shift in Position of Equilibrium	Reason
Increase in pressure	Shifts to products	Less moles of gas on product side (2) than the reactant side (4), so pressure is reduced by shifting to the product side Result: more ammonia produced
Increase in temperature	Shifts to reactants	Backward reaction is endothermic, so removes heat by shifting to the reactants Result: less ammonia produced
Increase in concentration of nitrogen and/ or hydrogen	Shifts to products	Less nitrogen and hydrogen on products side Result: more ammonia produced
Increase in concentration of ammonia	Shifts to reactants	Less ammonia on reactants side Result: less ammonia produced
Adding a catalyst	None	Catalyst only increases the speed that equilibrium is established, not its position Result: no change in amount of ammonia produced

2. The second example is the synthesis of hydrogen iodide.

$$H_{2(g)} + I_{2(g)} \rightleftarrows 2HI_{(g)}$$

$\Delta H = +51$ kJ mol^{-1} (i.e., endothermic, where heat is a "reactant")

Remembering that the equilibrium will shift to oppose any change (i.e., it will do the *opposite* of the imposed change), we can predict the changes in equilibrium position when changes are made.

Summary of Changes in Equilibrium Position When Conditions Are Changed in Synthesis of HI

Change in External Factor	Shift in Position of Equilibrium	Reason
Increase in pressure	None	Same moles of gas on product side and reactant side (2), so shift would not create any change in pressure Result: no change in amount of HI produced
Increase in temperature	Shifts to products	Forward reaction is endothermic, so removes heat by shifting to the products side Result: more HI produced
Increase in concentration of hydrogen and/or iodine	Shifts to products	Less hydrogen and iodine on products side Result: more HI produced
Increase in concentration of hydrogen iodide	Shifts to reactants	Less hydrogen iodide on reactant side Result: less HI produced
Adding a catalyst	None	Catalyst only increases the speed with which equilibrium is established, not its position Result: no change in amount of HI produced

Test Tip

Values of equilibrium constants are fixed at constant temperature, meaning that if the temperature does not change, neither does the value of K. Look out for this concept in questions on the test.

RATES OF REACTION (CHEMICAL KINETICS)

I. **RATES OF REACTION AND COLLISION THEORY—**
Different chemical reactions can occur at significantly
different rates. The basis for the study of the rate of
chemical reactions (kinetics) is *collision theory.*

A. COLLISION THEORY

1. Successful collisions (ones that lead to a reaction) only occur
   if three criteria are met.
   - i. The reactants come into contact (i.e., they collide).
   - ii. The collision occurs with a certain minimum energy,
     known as the *activation energy* (E_{act}).
   - iii. The collision has the correct collision geometry. This
     means that the reactants must collide in a certain
     physical orientation for a reaction to take place.
2. Any collision that does not fulfill all of these criteria will be
   unsuccessful—i.e., it will not lead to a reaction.

B. MEASURING RATES

1. A *rate* is some aspect of a reaction monitored as a function
   of time. Following are the two options when measuring
   rates. The choice is motivated by practical considerations
   for any given reaction and will be different for each unique
   situation.
   - i. Monitor the speed at which products are produced.
   - ii. Monitor the speed at which reactants are used up.

II. FACTORS CONTROLLING RATE OF REACTION

A. CONCENTRATION

1. Increasing the concentration of reactants (by putting more reactants into the same space) increases the collision frequency, leading to a faster rate of reaction.

2. The concentrations of the reactants in a gaseous reaction can be increased by increasing their pressure. Increases in pressure can be achieved by reducing the volume while leaving the amount of gas the same.

B. TEMPERATURE

1. An increase in temperature will result in an increased rate of reaction.

2. At higher temperatures, the average energy of the particles is greater and a greater number of particles will have energies $> E_{act}$. See the following diagram.

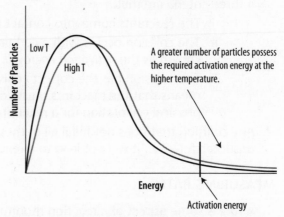

3. In addition, as the temperature increases so will the frequency of collisions, leading to more, successful collisions.

C. SOLID PARTICLE SIZE

1. When a solid reacts, only the particles on the surface of the solid are available for reaction.

2. If the solid is broken up into smaller pieces, its surface area increases and more particles are available for collision; therefore, the reaction rate increases.

D. CATALYSIS

1. *Catalysts* are substances that increase the rate of a reaction while remaining chemically unchanged.
2. Catalysts work by providing an alternative reaction pathway that requires a lower activation energy.
3. With a lower activation energy, a greater number of particles will possess the required, minimum energy (E_{act}) and a greater number of collisions will be successful. See the following diagrams.

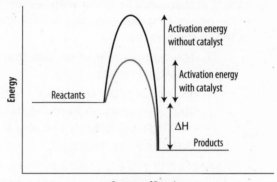

Note carefully that the addition of a catalyst does not change the ΔH value for the reaction (see Chapter 33), and that both the rate of the forward and the backward reaction will be increased when using a catalyst.

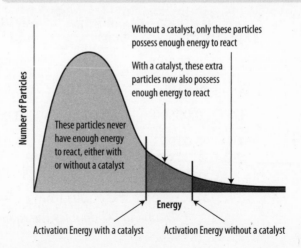

III. **THE RATE LAW AND ORDERS OF REACTION**

A. THE RATE LAW

1. *Rate law format.* The rate law (or rate equation) for a chemical reaction is used to express rates in a quantitative manner. It takes the following format: rate $= k [A]^x [B]^y [C]^z$....... and so on. In this format, k is the rate constant, [ ] represents concentration, and x, y, and z are the orders with respect to the reactants A, B, and C.

2. *Orders of reaction.* The order with respect to a given reactant is the power to which the concentration of that reactant is raised in the rate law.

    i. The overall order of the reaction is the sum of the individual orders.

    ii. It is not possible to deduce anything about the order of a reaction from the balanced chemical equation. Orders must be found experimentally.

    iii. Orders can be fractional.

3. *Example of using initial rate data to find the rate law.* Consider the following data for the reaction between X, Y, and Z. Deduce the orders of reaction with respect to each reactant, the overall order, the rate equation, and a value and units for the rate constant.

Using Initial Rate Data to Determine Orders

Expt.	Starting [X] in M	Starting [Y] in M	Starting [Z] in M	Rate in M min^{-1}
1	0.00500	0.0250	0.0250	10.0
2	0.0100	0.0250	0.0250	20.0
3	0.00500	0.0125	0.0250	10.0
4	0.0100	0.0250	0.0500	80.0

    i. The first method is inspection.

      a) Compare the results from experiment 1 and 2.

        ▶ *Doubling [X] doubles the rate.*

- ▸ *Other concentrations are kept constant to ensure a fair test.*
- ▸ *Therefore, the rate $\propto$ [X] and the rate are said to be first order with respect to [X].*

b) Compare the results from experiments (3) and (1).

- ▸ *Doubling [Y] does nothing to the rate.*
- ▸ *Other concentrations are kept constant to ensure a fair test.*
- ▸ *Therefore, the rate does not depend upon [Y] and the rate is said to be zero-order with respect to [Y].*

c) Compare the results from experiments (2) and (4).

- ▸ *Doubling [Z] quadruples the rate.*
- ▸ *Other concentrations are kept constant to ensure a fair test.*
- ▸ *Therefore, the rate $\propto [Z]^2$ and the rate are said to be second order with respect to [Z].*

ii. The second method is the mathematical treatment of initial rate data.

a) By comparing experiments 2 and 1, we find the following.

$$\frac{\text{Rate}_{\text{Expt. 2}} = 20.0 = k\,[0.0100]^{x}\,[0.0250]^{y}\,[0.0250]^{z}}{\text{Rate}_{\text{Expt. 1}} = 10.0 = k\,[0.00500]^{x}\,[0.0250]^{y}\,[0.0250]^{z}}$$

- ▸ *In this equation, x, y, and z are the orders with respect to [X], [Y], and [Z], respectively, and k is the rate constant.*
- ▸ *This allows the simplification of the expression to read as follows:*

$$\frac{\text{Rate}_{\text{Expt. 2}} = 20.0 = k\,[0.0100]^{x}\,\cancel{[0.0250]}^{\cancel{y}}\,\cancel{[0.0250]}^{\cancel{z}}}{\text{Rate}_{\text{Expt. 1}} = 10.0 = k\,[0.00500]^{x}\,\cancel{[0.0250]}^{\cancel{y}}\,\cancel{[0.0250]}^{\cancel{z}}} = 2 = 2^{x}$$

- ▸ *Therefore, x = 1—i.e., the order with respect to [X] is 1.*

b) By comparing experiments 1 and 3, we find the following.

$$\frac{\text{Rate}_{\text{Expt. 1}} = 10.0 = k\,[0.00500]^X\,[0.0250]^Y\,[0.0250]^Z}{\text{Rate}_{\text{Expt. 3}} = 10.0 = k\,[0.00500]^X\,[0.0125]^Y\,[0.0250]^Z}$$

▸ *In this equation, x, y, and z are the orders with respect to [X], [Y], and [Z], respectively, and k is the rate constant.*

▸ *This allows the simplification of the expression to read as follows:*

$$\frac{\text{Rate}_{\text{Expt. 1}} = 10.0 = k\,\cancel{[0.00500]}^{\,X}\,[0.0250]^Y\,\cancel{[0.0250]}^{\,Z}}{\text{Rate}_{\text{Expt. 3}} = 10.0 = k\,\cancel{[0.00500]}^{\,X}\,[0.0125]^Y\,\cancel{[0.0250]}^{\,Z}} = 1 = 2^y$$

▸ *Therefore, y = 0—i.e., the order with respect to [Y] is 0.*

c) By comparing experiments 2 and 4, we find the following.

$$\frac{\text{Rate}_{\text{Expt. 2}} = 20.0 = k\,[0.0100]^X\,[0.0250]^Y\,[0.0250]^Z}{\text{Rate}_{\text{Expt. 4}} = 80.0 = k\,[0.0100]^X\,[0.0250]^Y\,[0.0500]^Z}$$

▸ *In this equation, x, y, and z are the orders with respect to [X], [Y], and [Z], respectively, and k is the rate constant.*

▸ *This allows the simplification of the expression to read as follows:*

$$\frac{\text{Rate}_{\text{Expt. 2}} = 20.0 = k\,\cancel{[0.0100]}^{\,X}\,\cancel{[0.0250]}^{\,Y}\,[0.0250]^Z}{\text{Rate}_{\text{Expt. 4}} = 80.0 = k\,\cancel{[0.0100]}^{\,X}\,\cancel{[0.0250]}^{\,Y}\,[0.0500]^Z} = 0.25 = 0.5^z$$

▸ *Therefore, z = 2—i.e., the order with respect to [Z] is 2.*

iii. Combining the results from either the first or second method, gives rate $\propto [X]^1 [Y]^0 [Z]^2$ and by introducing the rate constant (k) and mathematically "tidying," the equation becomes rate $= k [X]^1[Z]^2$. So the overall order is $1 + 2 = 3$.

iv. Using this rate law, plug in data from experiment 1 to find k and its units.

$$10.0 \text{ M min}^{-1} = k (0.00500 \text{ M})^1 (0.0250 \text{ M})^2$$
$$k = 3.20 \times 10^6 \text{ M}^{-2} \text{ min}^{-1}$$

Test Tip

The units of rate constants can vary dramatically and should always be considered carefully on a case-by-case, question-by-question basis.

PART VII:

THERMOCHEMISTRY

CALORIMETRY AND SPECIFIC HEAT

I. SPECIFIC HEAT CAPACITY

A. DEFINITION

1. The specific heat of a substance can be defined as the energy required to raise 1 g of that substance by 1°C (1 K).

B. CALCULATIONS

1. Calculations involving specific heat use the equation $q = m \, c \, \Delta T$, where q = energy, m = mass, c = specific heat capacity, and ΔT = temperature change.
2. Following is an example calculation.
    i. If 30.0 grams of silver absorbs 375 J of energy, and the initial temperature of the silver is 23.0°C, calculate the final temperature of the silver. The specific heat capacity of silver = 0.235 J/g°C.

$$q = m \, c \, \Delta T$$
$$375 \text{ J} = (30.0 \text{ g}) (0.235 \text{ J/g°C}) (\Delta T)$$
$$\Delta T = 53.2°C$$

Because the energy was absorbed, the temperature of the silver went up, so the final temperature = 23.0 + 53.2 = 76.2°C.

Test Tip

Because ΔT represents a change in temperature, and a change of 1 K is the same as a change of 1°C, then the units of temperature are interchangeable in these problems.

CALORIMETRY

A. COFFEE-CUP CALORIMETRY

1. Styrofoam cups are commonly used as insulated containers in school laboratories for calculations involving specific heat capacities. See the following diagram.

B. EXAMPLE CALCULATION

1. If 5.00 g of urea are added to 90.00 g of water in a coffee-cup calorimeter, the temperature of the contents of the cup falls by 3.100°C. If the specific heat capacity of the solution is 4.184 J/g°C, calculate the energy change in the coffee cup.

$$q = m \, c \, \Delta T$$
$$q = (95.00 \text{ g}) (4.184 \text{ J/g°C}) (3.100°C)$$
$$q = 1232 \text{ J}$$

Test Tip

Sometimes questions may ask for the energy change, q, to be expressed in units of J mol^{-1} or kJ mol^{-1}. As such, be aware for the possible need for some simple unit conversions. Also, the specific heat capacity of water (4.184 J/g°C) is a very common value in these types of calculation; it helps if you can recognize it as such, and know that water has an unusually high specific heat capacity caused by hydrogen bonding (see Chapter 9).

ENTHALPY CHANGES AND **HESS'S LAW**

 ENTHALPY

A. DEFINITION

1. Every substance is said to have a heat content or *enthalpy*. Enthalpy is given the symbol, H. Most chemical reactions involve an enthalpy change, ΔH, where

$$\Delta H = \Sigma H_{f \text{ PRODUCTS}} - \Sigma H_{f \text{ REACTANTS}}$$

and where H_f represents the enthalpy of formation.

B. ENTHALPY-LEVEL DIAGRAMS

1. The enthalpy change can be illustrated using enthalpy-level diagrams.

   i. *ENDOTHERMIC reactions.* Enthalpy of products > enthalpy of reactants, and ΔH is positive, which means that energy must be put into the reaction for it to occur. See the following diagram.

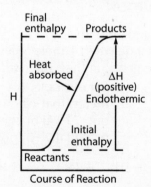

ii. *EXOTHERMIC reactions.* Enthalpy of products <
enthalpy of reactants, and ΔH is negative, which
means that energy is released from the reaction as it
occurs. See the following diagram.

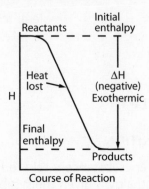

Course of Reaction

C. STANDARD STATES

1. Enthalpy changes are usually measured under standard
conditions:
   i. All gases at 1 atm pressure
   ii. All solutions at 1 M concentration
   iii. Temperature at 298.15 K

II. STANDARD ENTHALPY OF FORMATION (ΔH_f^θ)

A. DEFINITION

1. Standard enthalpy of formation is defined as the enthalpy
change when 1 mole of a substance is formed from its
elements, in their standard states.
   i. For example, $\Delta H_f^\theta [C_2H_5OH_{(l)}] = -279$ kJmol^{-1}
   means that when the following reaction is carried
   out, 279 kJ of energy are released. ΔH_f^θ values may
   be negative or positive:

$$2C_{(graphite)} + 3H_{2(g)} + \tfrac{1}{2}O_{2(g)} \rightarrow C_2H_5OH_{(l)} \qquad \Delta H^\theta = -279 \text{ kJmol}^{-1}$$

III. STANDARD ENTHALPY OF COMBUSTION (ΔH_c^{θ})

A. DEFINITION

1. Standard enthalpy of *combustion* is defined as the enthalpy change when 1 mole of a substance is completely burned in oxygen. Because energy is released in a combustion reaction, ΔH_c^{θ} will be negative.

   i. For example, $\Delta H_c^{\theta} [C_2H_{6(g)}] = -1565$ kJmol^{-1} means that when the following reaction is carried out, 1565 kJ of energy are released:

$$C_2H_{6(g)} + 3\tfrac{1}{2}O_{2(g)} \rightarrow 2CO_{2(g)} + 3H_2O_{(l)} \qquad \Delta H^{\theta} = -1565 \text{ kJmol}^{-1}$$

Test Tip

It is useful to remember that compounds containing some combination of carbon, hydrogen, and oxygen, when completely burned in air (O_2), produce carbon dioxide and water only. The combustion of other reactants may require other knowledge or intelligent guesswork to determine the products of that combustion.

IV. HESS'S LAW

A. DEFINITION

1. Hess's law states that the enthalpy change during a reaction depends only on the nature of the reactants and products and is independent of the route taken.

B. EXAMPLE CALCULATION

1. Calculate the standard enthalpy of combustion of propan-2-ol ($CH_3CH(OH)CH_3$), given the following data: enthalpies of combustion for $C_{(graphite)} = -393$ kJmol^{-1} and $H_{2(g)} = -286$ kJmol^{-1} and the enthalpy of formation of propan-2-ol $= -318$ kJmol^{-1}.

   i. Identify the "target" equation—i.e., the enthalpy change that the question requires you to calculate.

$$CH_3CH(OH)CH_3 + 4\tfrac{1}{2}O_2 \rightarrow 3CO_2 + 4H_2O$$

ii. Convert data given to chemical equations.

Equation a. $C + O_2 \rightarrow CO_2$ $\Delta H = -393 \text{ kJmol}^{-1}$

Equation b. $H_2 + \frac{1}{2}O_2 \rightarrow H_2O$ $\Delta H = -286 \text{ kJmol}^{-1}$

Equation c. $3C + 4H_2 + \frac{1}{2}O_2 \rightarrow$ $\Delta H = -318 \text{ kJmol}^{-1}$
$CH_3CH(OH)CH_3$

iii. Manipulate the data equations to create the "target" equation. Because the target needs $3CO_2$ on the product side, multiply equation (a) by 3 and the enthalpy change for equation (a) by 3:

$3C + 3O_2 \rightarrow 3CO_2$ $\Delta H = 3(-393 \text{ kJmol}^{-1})$

Because the target needs $4H_2O$ on the product side, multiply equation (b) by 4 and the enthalpy change for equation (b) by 4:

$4H_2 + 2O_2 \rightarrow 4H_2O$ $\Delta H = 4(-286 \text{ kJmol}^{-1})$

Because the target needs propan-2-ol on reactant side, reverse equation (c) and reverse the sign of the enthalpy change for equation (c):

$CH_3CH(OH)CH_3 \rightarrow 3C + 4H_2 + \frac{1}{2}O_2$ $\Delta H = (-1)(-318 \text{ kJmol}^{-1})$

SUM the preceding equations and enthalpy changes to give:

$CH_3CH(OH)CH_3 + 4\frac{1}{2}O_2 \rightarrow 3CO_2 + 4H_2O$ $\Delta H = -2005 \text{ kJmol}^{-1}$

Test Tip

Work backwards from the target equation to give clues as to how to manipulate each data equation. Remember to multiply ALL components of each data equation by the multiplier, and that reversing equations changes the sign for ΔH. Also, since O_2 appears in the target equation AND in all three data equations, it is best not to try and manipulate the data to accommodate it. If manipulated correctly, the O_2 will take care of itself in the final equation.

HEATING AND COOLING CURVES

I. HEATING CURVES

A. WHAT ARE THEY?

1. *Heating curves* are plots of temperature against time (at constant pressure) that result when heating a solid substance through its melting and boiling points until it becomes a heated gas.

B. INTERPRETING THE HEATING CURVE

1. Starting with a solid below its melting point, the following is observed.

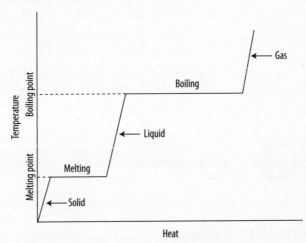

i. The temperature of the solid increases at a constant rate until it begins to melt.

   ii. When melting begins, the temperature is constant until the solid has all turned to liquid.

   iii. The temperature of the liquid increases at a constant rate until it begins to boil.

   iv. When boiling begins, the temperature is constant until the liquid has all turned to gas.

   v. The temperature of the gas increases at a constant rate.

   vi. In the regions where the temperature of the solid, liquid, or gas is being increased, the amount of energy being added can be calculated using $q = m\, c\, \Delta T$, where m is mass, c is the specific heat capacity of the substance being heated, and ΔT is the temperature change.

     a) *Standard enthalpy of fusion.* This is energy change when 1 mole of a substance is converted from a solid to a liquid. Where the solid is melting, the amount of energy being added can be calculated using $q = (\Delta H_{fusion})(moles)$.

     b) *Standard enthalpy of vaporization.* This is energy change when 1 mole of a substance is converted from a liquid to a gas. Where the liquid is boiling, the amount of energy being added can be calculated using $q = (\Delta H_{vaporization})(moles)$.

     c) **These are endothermic processes because energy must be added.**

   vii. A *plateau region* represents a stage when two phases are in equilibrium with one another.

Test Tip

Here is a helpful way to understand the process: the energy being added is either being used to increase temperature OR is being used to effect a phase change—not both.

II. COOLING CURVES

A. WHAT ARE THEY?

1. Cooling curves are plots of temperature against time (at constant pressure) that result when cooling a gaseous

substance through its condensation and freezing points until it becomes a cooled solid.

B. INTERPRETING THE COOLING CURVE

1. Starting with a gas above its boiling point, the following is observed (see the following diagram):

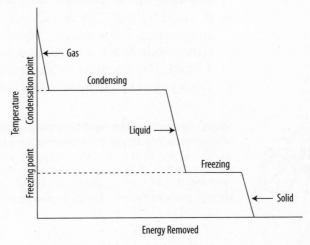

i. The temperature of the gas decreases at a constant rate until it begins to condense.

ii. When condensing begins, the temperature is constant until the gas has all turned to liquid.

iii. The temperature of the liquid decreases at a constant rate until it begins to freeze.

iv. When freezing begins, the temperature is constant until the liquid has all turned to solid.

v. The temperature of the solid decreases at a constant rate.

vi. In the regions where the temperature of the solid, liquid, or gas is being decreased, the amount of energy being removed can be calculated using $q = m\,c\,\Delta T$, where m is mass, c is the specific heat capacity of the substance being heated, and ΔT is the temperature change.

  a) Where the gas is condensing, the amount of energy being removed can be calculated using $q = (\Delta H_{vaporization})(moles)$.

b) Where the liquid is freezing, the amount of energy being removed can be calculated using $q = (\Delta H_{fusion})(moles)$.

c) **These are exothermic processes because energy must be removed.**

vii. A plateau region represents a stage when two phases are in equilibrium with one another.

viii. It is possible that some liquids may exhibit *supercooling*. This is where a liquid is cooled to a temperature below its melting point but remains a liquid. This is a meta-stable state from which solidification can be initiated by shaking or seeding.

Any exothermic process must be accompanied by an equivalent endothermic process, so if a substance is losing energy and cooling down, then that energy must be transferred to the surroundings, which will be gaining energy and heating up (and vice versa). This is an application of the law of conservation of energy and can be summarized as energy lost = energy gained.

ENTROPY

I. ENTROPY

A. DEFINITION

1. *Entropy* can be described as the degree of disorder or degree of randomness. It is given the symbol S, and has the units J/Kmol. Where there is an increase in entropy—i.e., an increase in disorder—ΔS is assigned a positive value.

B. ABSOLUTE ENTROPIES

1. Every substance has its own value for absolute entropy.
    i. The third law of thermodynamics states that the entropy of a pure, perfect crystal at absolute zero is = 0 J/Kmol. Because all substances exist in the real world at temperatures greater than absolute zero, they are all more disordered and hence they all have positive absolute entropies (i.e., absolute entropies greater than zero).
    ii. Gases have absolute entropies that are significantly greater than the absolute entropies of liquids, which in turn have greater absolute entropies than solids.
    iii. Absolute entropies are greater in more complex molecules.
    iv. For example $I_{2(s)}$ has an absolute entropy = 116 J/Kmol, $Br_{2(l)}$ = 152 J/Kmol, $Cl_{2(g)}$ = 223 J/Kmol, and $ClF_{3(g)}$ = 282 J/Kmol.

C. CHANGES IN ENTROPY IN CHEMICAL REACTIONS

1. Predictions based upon state symbols are as follows.

   i. In the reaction, $Na_2CO_{3(s)} \rightarrow Na_2O_{(s)} + CO_{2(g)}$, 1 mole of solid forms 1 mole of solid and 1 mole of gas. Because gases have large entropies when compared to solids, entropy (disorder) increases and ΔS is positive.

   ii. In the reaction, $MgO_{(s)} + H_2O_{(l)} \rightarrow Mg(OH)_{2(s)}$, 1 mole of solid and 1 mole of liquid form 1 mole of solid. Because liquids have large entropies when compared to solids, entropy (disorder) decreases and ΔS is negative.

2. Calculations use the following equation:

$$\Delta S^{\theta}_{REACTION} \quad S^{\theta}_{PRODUCTS} \quad S^{\theta}_{REACTANTS}$$

   i. Calculate the change in entropy for the following reaction, given the absolute entropies provided:

$$N_{2(g)} + 3H_{2(g)} \rightarrow 2NH_{3(g)}$$

   Absolute entropies: 193 J/K mol for $NH_{3(g)}$, 192 J/K mol for $N_{2(g)}$ and 131 J/K mol for $H_{2(g)}$

$$\Delta S^{\theta}_{REACTION} = [(2)(193)] - [192 + (3)(131)]$$
$$= -199 \text{ J/K mol}$$

II. SPONTANEITY

A. SPONTANEITY IS THE MEASURE OF HOW LIKELY A CHEMICAL REACTION IS TO OCCUR. IN A SPONTANEOUS REACTION, THE TOTAL ENTROPY MUST INCREASE

1. *Total entropy* is calculated using $\Delta S_{TOTAL} = \Delta S_{REACTION} + \Delta S_{SURROUNDINGS}$,

   and $\Delta S^{\theta}_{REACTION} \quad S^{\theta}_{PRODUCTS} \quad S^{\theta}_{REACTANTS}$,

   and $\Delta S_{SURROUNDINGS} \quad \dfrac{\Delta H \cdot}{T}$

2. Rather than considering total entropy, it is more common to consider only *entropy of reaction* as a guide to spontaneity. Enthalpy and entropy for reactions are brought together in the Gibbs free energy equation.

III. GIBBS FREE ENERGY, ENTROPY, AND ENTHALPY

A. THE ROLE OF ENTHALPY IN SPONTANEITY

1. Exothermic reactions (i.e., those with a decrease in enthalpy and a negative ΔH) tend to be more likely to occur.
2. Exothermic reactions have products that are more stable than their reactants.

B. THE ROLE OF ENTROPY IN SPONTANEITY

1. Reactions with an increase in entropy (i.e., those with a positive ΔS) tend to be more likely to occur.
2. The universe tends toward a state of greater disorder (second law of thermodynamics).

C. GIBBS FREE ENERGY

1. Despite the preceding predictions, we find that some endothermic reactions (positive ΔH) are spontaneous, and also some reactions with a negative ΔS are spontaneous. This means we must consider both enthalpy and entropy when predicting spontaneity.
2. The Gibbs free energy equation calculates the amount of energy that can be used for work and is calculated using the following formula:

$$\Delta G^{\theta} \quad \Delta H^{\theta} \quad T\Delta S^{\theta}_{REACTION}$$

Test Tip

When using the Gibbs free energy equation, ensure that units for ΔH and ΔS are the same (either both in J or both in kJ) before performing the calculation.

A value for Gibbs free energy can be calculated in much the same way as enthalpy and entropy by using the following formula:

$$\Delta G^{\theta} \quad G^{\theta}_{f\,PRODUCTS} \quad G^{\theta}_{f\,REACTANTS}$$

3. Following is the relationship between Gibbs free energy and spontaneity.

    i. If ΔG is negative, then the reaction is spontaneous.

    ii. If ΔG is positive, then the reaction is nonspontaneous.

    iii. If ΔG is zero, then the reaction is at equilibrium.

Combinations of Enthalpy and Entropy and the Corresponding Value of Gibbs Free Energy

ΔH	$\Delta S_{reaction}$	ΔG
+	+	− at high temperatures + at low temperatures
+	−	+
−	+	−
−	−	− at low temperatures + at high temperatures

In chemistry, the word spontaneous *does not mean that a reaction will necessarily* instantaneously *occur, rather it means that it is considered* feasible*. A feasible (spontaneous) reaction may still be a very slow one, IF the energy of activation is very high. In short, reactions described as* spontaneous, *in this sense, may not literally be spontaneous.*

4. Gibbs free energy can be calculated from the equilibrium constant using $\Delta G^{\theta} = -RT \ln K$, where R = universal gas constant, ln K is the natural log of the equilibrium constant at temperature T (in Kelvin).

PART VIII:

DESCRIPTIVE CHEMISTRY

INORGANIC DESCRIPTIVE CHEMISTRY

I. NOMENCLATURE OF IONS AND COMPOUNDS

A. BINARY COMPOUNDS OF METALS AND NONMETALS (IONIC COMPOUNDS)

1. These are formed between one monatomic metal ion and one monatomic nonmetal ion.
2. Positive and negative charges must be balanced—i.e., there must be no net charge.
3. *Naming.* The unmodified name of the positive ion is written first, followed by the root of the negative element with the ending modified to "–ide."

Some Common Monatomic Ions

Negative Ions (ANIONS)			Positive Ions (CATIONS)		
Name	Charge	Symbol	Name	Charge	Symbol
Bromide	1–	Br^-	Aluminum	3+	Al^{3+}
Chloride	1–	Cl^-	Barium	2+	Ba^{2+}
Fluoride	1–	F^-	Calcium	2+	Ca^{2+}
Hydride	1–	H^-	Copper (I), (II)	1+, 2+	Cu^+, Cu^{2+}
Iodide	1–	I^-	Hydrogen	1+	H^+
Nitride	3–	N^{3-}	Iron (II), (III)	2+, 3+	Fe^{2+}, Fe^{3+}
Oxide	2–	O^{2-}	Lead (II), (IV)	2+, 4+	Pb^{2+}, Pb^{4+}

(continued)

Some Common Monatomic Ions (*continued*)

Negative Ions (ANIONS)			Positive Ions (CATIONS)		
Name	Charge	Symbol	Name	Charge	Symbol
Phosphide	3−	P^{3-}	Lithium	1+	Li^+
Sulfide	2−	S^{2-}	Magnesium	2+	Mg^{2+}
			Potassium	1+	K^+
			Silver	1+	Ag^+
			Sodium	1+	Na^+
			Tin (II), (IV)	2+, 4+	Sn^{2+}, Sn^{4+}
			Zinc	2+	Zn^{2+}

4. Some metal ions (often those of transition metals) include a Roman numeral after their name. This denotes that they have varying positive charges and the numeral identifies the charge.

5. Examples of binary ionic compounds include NaCl sodium chloride, AlN (aluminum nitride), $BaCl_2$ (barium chloride), K_2O (potassium oxide), CuO (copper (II) oxide), and Cu_2O (copper (I) oxide).

B. BINARY ACIDS

1. Binary acids are formed with the hydrogen ion, H^+, and a monatomic negative ion.

2. Positive and negative charges must be balanced—i.e., there must be no net charge.

3. *Naming.* The prefix "hydro" is followed by the negative ion name modified to an "–ic" ending.

4. Examples of binary acids include HCl (hydrochloric acid) and HF (hydrofluoric acid).

C. POLYATOMIC IONS AND COMPOUNDS CONTAINING POLYATOMIC IONS

1. Polyatomic ions are those where more than one element is combined to create a species with a charge.

Common Polyatomic Ions

Name	Charge	Formula
Ammonium	1+	NH_4^+
Carbonate	2−	CO_3^{2-}
Chromate (VI)	2−	CrO_4^{2-}
Dichromate (VI)	2−	$Cr_2O_7^{2-}$
Ethanedioate (oxalate)	2−	$C_2O_4^{2-}$
Hydrogen carbonate	1−	HCO_3^-
Hydrogen sulfate	1−	HSO_4^-
Hydroxide	1−	OH^-
Manganate (VII) (permanganate)	1−	MnO_4^-
Nitrate	1−	NO_3^-
Nitrite	1−	NO_2^-
Phosphate	3−	PO_4^{3-}
Phosphite	3−	PO_3^{3-}
Sulfate	2−	SO_4^{2-}
Sulfite	2−	SO_3^{2-}

Test Tip

You have to learn the names and formulae of common poly-atomic ions. At the high school level, this is just some good old-fashioned legwork, but there are a couple of patterns that may help. Where (amongst the common polyatomic ions stud-ied in high school) there are only two members in a series, the endings are "–ite" and "–ate." For example, at the high school level, typical polyatomic ions that come in pairs are those of sulfur in sulfite, SO_3^{2-} and sulfate, SO_4^{2-}; those of nitrogen in nitrite, NO_2^- and nitrate, NO_3^-; and those of phosphorous in phosphite, PO_3^{3-} and phosphate, PO_4^{3-}. When there are four members in a series, the "hypo-" and "per-" prefixes are used in addition to "-ite" and "-ate" endings. An example is those of bromine, in hypobromite (BrO^-), bromite (BrO_2^-), bromate (BrO_3^-), and perbromate (BrO_4^-).

2. Positive and negative charges must be balanced—i.e., there must be no net charge.

3. *Naming.* The unmodified name of the positive ion is written first, followed by the unmodified name of the negative ion.

4. Examples of ionic compounds containing polyatomic ions include K_2CO_3 (potassium carbonate), NH_4NO_3 (ammonium nitrate), $Zn(HSO_4)_2$ (zinc hydrogen sulfate), $Al_2(SO_4)_3$ (aluminum sulfate), and $NaClO_4$ (sodium perchlorate).

D. POLYATOMIC ACIDS

1. Polyatomic acids are formed between hydrogen ions, H^+, and polyatomic anions.

2. Positive and negative charges must be balanced—i.e., there must be no net charge.

3. *Naming.* Use the name of the polyatomic ion and replace an "-ite" ending with "–ous," or an "-ate" ending with "–ic." Then add the word, "acid."

4. Examples of acids of polyatomic ions include HClO (hypochlor*ous acid*, from the hypochlor*ite* ion, ClO^-) and $HClO_4$ (perchlor*ic acid*, from the perchlor*ate* ion, ClO_4^-).

E. BINARY COMPOUNDS OF TWO NONMETALS (MOLECULES)

1. Binary molecular compounds formed between two nonmetals.

2. No ions are present, so there are no charge considerations.

3. *Naming.* The unmodified name of the first element is followed by the root of the second element with the ending modified to "-ide."

4. Use the prefixes *mono, di, tri, tetra, penta,* and *hexa* to represent one, two, three, four, five, and six atoms of each element, respectively, but the *mono* prefix is only ever applied to the second element.

5. If the prefix ends with "a" or "o" and the element name begins with "a" or "o," then the final vowel of the prefix is often omitted.

6. Some compounds have trivial, or common, names that have come to supersede their systematic names; for example, "water," not "dihydrogen monoxide."

7. Examples of binary molecular compounds include SO_2 (sulfur dioxide), BCl_3 (boron trichloride), CO (carbon monoxide), and CCl_4 (carbon tetrachloride).

II. COLORS AND QUALITATIVE CHEMISTRY

A. FLAME TEST COLORS

1. Certain cations can be detected by conducting a flame test.

Flame Test Colors for Common Ions

Ion	Flame Color
Li^+, Sr^{2+}, Ca^{2+}	Red (various shades)
Na^+	Yellow/orange
K^+	Lilac
Ba^{2+}	Green
Cu^{2+}	Blue-green

B. TRANSITION METAL ION COLORS

1. In solution, many transition metals exhibit distinct colors.

Common Colors of Aqueous Transition Metals

Ion	Color in Solution
Cr^{3+}	Green
Cr^{6+}	Orange
Mn^{2+}	Pale pink
Mn^{7+}	Dark purple
Fe^{2+}	Green
Fe^{3+}	Red/brown

(continued)

Common Colors of Aqueous Transition Metals (*continued*)

Ion	Color in Solution
Ni^{2+}	Green
Cu^+	Colorless
Cu^{2+}	Blue
Zn^{2+}	Colorless

C. COMMON PRECIPITATE COLORS

1. Colors of precipitates can aid identification of compounds.
    i. White = AgCl, $BaSO_4$, $PbCl_2$ plus many precipitates of nontransition metal hydroxides, sulfates, and carbonates
    ii. Blue = many copper (II) precipitates
    iii. Yellow = AgI and PbI_2
    iv. Green = many iron (II) and nickel (II) precipitates
    v. Red/brown = many iron (III) precipitates

D. COMMON ACID–BASE INDICATOR COLORS

Common Colors of Acid–Base Indicators

Indicator	In Acid	In Base
Methyl orange	Red	Yellow
Methyl red	Red	Yellow
Litmus	Red	Blue
Universal	Red	Blue/purple
Phenolphthalein	Colorless	Pink

E. MISCELLANEOUS COLORS

1. Elements: fluorine gas (pale yellow/green), chlorine gas (green), bromine liquid (orange/brown), and iodine solid (dark purple)
2. Other: ammonia (NH_3) turns red litmus paper blue, gives dense white fumes in contact with concentrated HCl fumes, NO_2 gas (orange/brown)

ORGANIC CHEMISTRY

 I. **ORGANIC CHEMISTRY**

A. WHAT IS IT?

1. *Organic chemistry* involves the study of compounds of carbon. There are many compounds containing carbon and hydrogen only and millions of other organic compounds containing carbon, hydrogen, and other elements such as nitrogen, oxygen, sulfur, and the halogens.

 II. **HYDROCARBONS AND NOMENCLATURE**

A. HYDROCARBONS

1. A *hydrocarbon* is a compound containing hydrogen and carbon only. Following are three common types.
    i. Alkanes with the general formula C_nH_{2n+2} that contain all single bonds (organic compounds that contain all single bonds are said to be *saturated*)
    ii. Alkenes with the general formula C_nH_{2n} that contain carbon–carbon double bonds (organic compounds that contain double or triple bonds are said to be *unsaturated*)
    iii. Alkynes with the general formula C_nH_{2n-2} that contain carbon–carbon triple bonds (organic compounds that contain double or triple bonds are said to be *unsaturated*)

    (In all of the preceding general formulae, n = the number of carbon atoms in the compound.)

Single bonds between atoms are called sigma (σ) bonds. A double bond is comprised of one sigma and one pi (π) bond, and a triple bond is comprised of one sigma and two pi bonds.

B. NOMENCLATURE—NAMING HYDROCARBONS

1. The root name of any organic compound is based upon the number of carbon atoms in the longest, continuous carbon chain.
2. The suffix (ending) is based upon the type of hydrocarbon. Alkanes have an "-ane" ending, alkenes "-ene," and alkynes "-yne."

Nomenclature of Hydrocarbons

NUMBER OF C ATOMS	ROOT	ALKANES	ALKENES	ALKYNES
1	meth-	Methane, CH_4	–	–
2	eth-	Ethane, C_2H_6	Ethene, C_2H_4	Ethyne, C_2H_2
3	prop-	Propane, C_3H_8	Propene, C_3H_6	Propyne, C_3H_4
4	but-	Butane, C_4H_{10}	Butene, C_4H_8	Butyne, C_4H_6
5	pent-	Pentane, C_5H_{12}	Pentene, C_5H_{10}	Pentyne, C_5H_8
6	hex-	Hexane, C_6H_{14}	Hexene, C_6H_{12}	Hexyne, C_6H_{10}
7	hept-	Heptane, C_7H_{16}	Heptene, C_7H_{14}	Heptyne, C_7H_{12}
8	oct-	Octane, C_8H_{18}	Octene, C_8H_{16}	Octyne, C_8H_{14}
9	non-	Nonane, C_9H_{20}	Nonene, C_9H_{18}	Nonyne, C_9H_{16}
10	dec-	Decane, $C_{10}H_{22}$	Decene, $C_{10}H_{20}$	Decyne, $C_{10}H_{18}$

III. OTHER FUNCTIONAL GROUPS

A. TYPES

1. When organic compounds contain atoms other than just carbon and hydrogen, other *functional groups* exist. A functional group is a specific group of atoms within an organic molecule that is responsible for the chemical properties of that molecule.

Functional Groups

Functional Groups		Example
General Name	**General Structure**	**Name and Formula**
Esters	O ‖ C R—C—O R	Ethyl ethanoate, $CH_3CO_2C_2H_5$
Carboxylic acids	O ‖ C R—C—OH	Ethanoic acid, CH_3CO_2H
Aldehydes	O ‖ C R—C—H	Propanal, CH_3CH_2CHO
Ketones	O ‖ C R—C—R	Propanone, CH_3COCH_3
Alcohols	R-OH	Ethanol, C_2H_5OH
Amines	R-NH$_2$	Ethylamine, $C_2H_5NH_2$
Halogens	R-X	Chloromethane, CH_3Cl

R = a carbon chain and X = halogen

IV. ISOMERISM AND ISOMERS

A. ISOMERISM

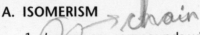

1. *Isomers* are compounds with the same molecular formula but different molecular structures or arrangements in space.
2. This can lead to a number of different structures with the same molecular formula.
3. The structures can have different functional groups, the same functional groups but with different bonds present, or different physical arrangements in space.
4. A compound that contains a carbon atom with four different groups attached to it can exhibit *optical* isomerism. These compounds have nonsuperimposable mirror images.

B. EXAMPLES OF PAIRS OF ISOMERS

1. Pentane and 2-methylbutane—both C_5H_{12}:

2. Butan-1-ol and butan-2-ol—both C_4H_9OH:

3. Propanal and propanone—both C_3H_6O:

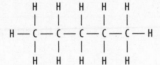

4. Optical isomers with nonsuperimposable mirror images—e.g., 1-choroethanol where a central carbon atom has (a) hydrogen, (b) methyl (CH_3), (c) hydroxyl (OH), and (d) chlorine attached—both C_2H_5OCl.

$$HO - \underset{\underset{H}{|}}{\overset{\overset{Cl}{|}}{C}} - CH_3$$

ENVIRONMENTAL CHEMISTRY AND NUCLEAR CHEMISTRY

I. ENVIRONMENTAL CHEMISTRY

> In this section, you will find very brief summaries of the chemistry of the main areas of environmental concern, but reading around the subject and having some solid general knowledge will increase your understanding and help even more. Try to be engaged and aware of chemistry outside of your formal studies such as in current affairs and the news. The more you do that, and the more you increase your chemical general knowledge, the better you are likely to do when it comes to test questions that deal with environmental issues.

A. ACID RAIN

1. Formation
   i. Burning fossil fuels release oxides of sulfur into the air, where they combine with water to form sulfurous and sulfuric acids.
   ii. Naturally occurring nitrogen in the air can be converted to oxides of nitrogen (e.g., when lightning occurs), where they combine with water to form nitrous and nitric acids.
   iii. Naturally occurring carbon dioxide in the air can combine with water to form carbonic acid.

2. Consequences
   i. Bodies of water become increasing acidic, in turn adversely affecting wildlife.
   ii. Soil and plants (especially forests) are damaged by acid rain.

        iii. Acid rain causes damage to, and erosion of, buildings, monuments, statues, and other structures, especially where certain metals or limestone/marble (calcium carbonate) have been used in construction.

B. OZONE DEPLETION

1. What is it?
   - i. Ozone, O_3 in the earth's stratosphere, absorbs high-energy radiation, which in turn, protects the Earth from potentially damaging ultraviolet radiation.
   - ii. Chemicals such as chlorofluorocarbons (CFCs) from refrigerants, aerosols, and other sources cause the breakdown and destruction of the ozone layer by converting O_3 to oxygen, O_2.
2. Consequences
   - i. One consequence is potential cellular damage to living organisms on Earth.

C. GREENHOUSE EFFECT AND GLOBAL WARMING

1. *Greenhouse effect.* Gases such as carbon dioxide (released as a consequence of burning hydrocarbons), absorb radiation reflected from the Earth and "trap" it in the atmosphere. As a result, radiation is kept close to the Earth and the temperature rises (like in a greenhouse).
2. *Global warming.* This refers to the rising average temperature of the Earth associated (in large part) with the increasing amounts of greenhouse gases.

Test Tip

It's good to know that the Earth's atmosphere is approximately 78% nitrogen, 21% oxygen, and 1% a mixture of argon, carbon dioxide, neon, methane, hydrogen, helium, and other gases.

D. HARD WATER

1. *Causes.* Naturally occurring deposits of calcium (Ca^{2+}) and magnesium (Mg^{2+}) ions in water make it "hard."

2. *Consequences.* The presence of calcium and magnesium ions can prevent soap from creating lather and can create "lime scale," a precipitate that can clog pipes and appliances, reducing efficiency.

3. *Treatment.* Exchanging the calcium and magnesium ions with sodium ions reduces the problems associated with hard water and the water is said to be "soft" or has been "softened."

II. NUCLEAR CHEMISTRY

A. RADIOACTIVITY IS THE SPONTANEOUS DECAY OF CERTAIN NUCLEI TO ACHIEVE GREATER STABILITY

1. There are three common types of radiation that result from radioactive decay.
   - i. alpha
   - ii. beta
   - iii. gamma

2. The properties of the types of radiation are summarized in the following table.

Summary of the Properties of Common Types of Radioactivity

	ALPHA α	BETA β	GAMMA γ
NATURE	A helium nucleus	Essentially electrons	High-energy and high-frequency electromagnetic radiation
CHARGE	+2	−1	0
MASS	4	$\dfrac{1}{1840}$	0
MOVEMENT IN ELECTRIC FIELD	Toward negative plate	Toward positive plate	None
PENETRATING POWER	Least	Intermediate	Greatest

B. RADIOACTIVITY (NUCLEAR) DECAY EQUATIONS

1. *Alpha* decay (the loss of a helium nucleus) is illustrated by the following equation.

$$^mX_n \rightarrow {}^{m-4}Y_{n-2} + {}^4\alpha_2$$

2. *Beta decay* (a neutron splits to give a proton and an electron) is illustrated by the following equation.

$$^mX_n \rightarrow {}^mZ_{n+1} + {}^0\beta_{-1}$$

3. *Gamma decay* (a rearrangement of the nuclear particles only) is illustrated by the following equation.

$$^mX_n \rightarrow {}^mX_n + {}^0\gamma_0$$

4. *Positron emission* (a positron has the same mass as an electron, but has a positive charge) is illustrated by the following equation.

$$^mX_n \rightarrow {}^mZ_{n-1} + {}^0\beta_{+1}$$

5. *Electron capture* (a captured electron combines with a proton in the nucleus to form a neutron) is illustrated by the following equation.

$$^mX_n + {}^0e_{-1} \rightarrow {}^mZ_{n-1}$$

Note: In every preceding equation in (1)–(5), m represents the mass number of the isotope, n represents the atomic number, and all equations must be balanced in terms of mass numbers and atomic numbers. When the atomic number changes, so does the element and hence a new symbol is used.

C. HALF-LIFE

1. The half-life of a radioactive nucleus is the time taken for half of the atoms to decay. It is independent of the initial quantity of atoms.
2. Following is an example calculation.

If it takes 18 days for a sample of a radioactive isotope to decay to one-eighth of its original mass, what is the half-life?

Use the formula, $\dfrac{1}{2^n}$ = fraction of radioactive material remaining after n half-lives $\dfrac{1}{2^n} = \dfrac{1}{8}$, so n = 3.

Because 18 days = 3 half-lives, one half-life = 6 days.

D. FISSION AND FUSION

1. *Nuclear fission* is the splitting of large, heavy nuclei into smaller ones.
2. *Nuclear fusion* is the fusing of two smaller nuclei to form one, heavier one.

PART IX:

LABORATORY

KNOWING YOUR WAY AROUND THE LABORATORY

I. LAB EQUIPMENT

A. SELECTION BASED UPON FUNCTION

It is quite common for test questions to ask you to match a piece of glassware or lab equipment to a particular function or purpose. You should become familiar with names and appearance of equipment in the following list, along with their function and role in the lab.

Name of Equipment	Picture	Function
Beaker		Glass used to hold and heat solutions. Not used for measuring.
Buchner Funnel		Used for suction filtration along with a filtering flask.

(continued)

(continued)

Name of Equipment	Picture	Function
Bunsen Burner		Produces a flame for heating.
Burette		Used for volumetric delivery of solutions. Used in titration experiment. Stopcock is small handle that controls the delivery of liquid.
Clamp and Ring Stand		Holds funnels, flasks, wire gauze for burning.

(continued)

(*continued*)

Name of Equipment	Picture	Function
Crucible	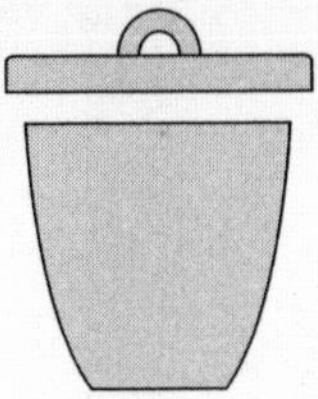	Heat resistant container used to heat compounds. Can be used in combination with ring stand and clamp.
Distillation Apparatus	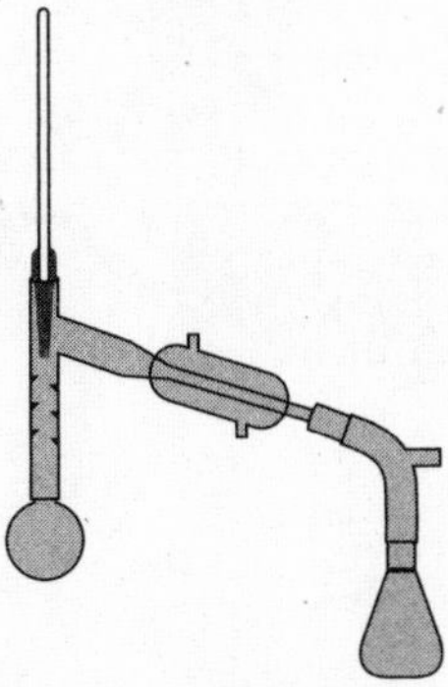	Used to separate a mixture of compounds based on boiling point.
Erlenmeyer Flask	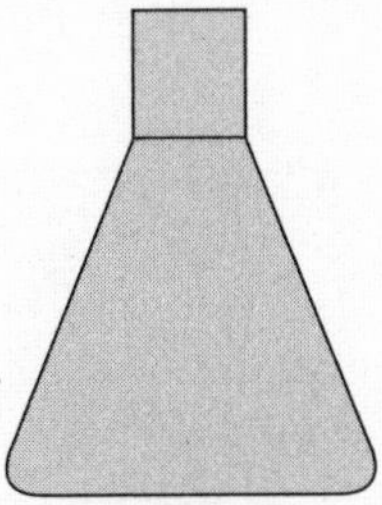	Conical piece of lab equipment that is used for holding liquids. Not used for measuring.
Filtering Flask	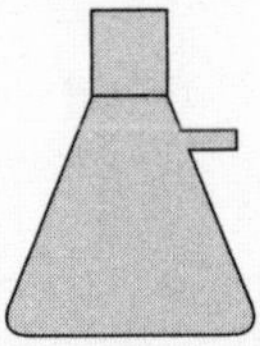	Used in combination vacuum suction and Buchner funnel.
Funnel	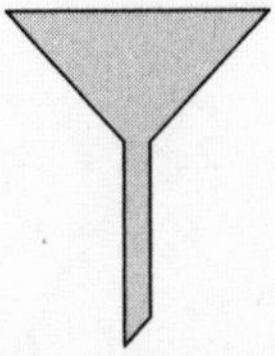	Along with filter paper can be used to separate solids from liquids.

(*continued*)

(*continued*)

Name of Equipment	Picture	Function
Graduated Cylinder		Used for the general measurement of liquids and solutions.
Hot Plate		Electric device that allows for controlled delivery of heat. Often contains a metallic stirrer to allow for mixing.
Mortar and Pestle		Porcelain piece of equipment that can be used for crushing and grinding.
Separatory Funnel		Allows for the separation of immiscible liquids.
Thermometer		Used to read temperature.

(*continued*)

(*continued*)

Name of Equipment	Picture	Function
Volumetric Flask		Used to accurately prepare solutions of various concentrations.
Volumetric Pipet		Used for measuring precise volumes of liquids and solutions, often in titrations.

II. MEASUREMENTS, ACCURACY, AND PRECISION

A. SIGNIFICANT FIGURES

1. Following is the process for determining the number of significant figures.

   i. Any *nonzero integers* are always counted as significant.

      a) 123 (3 sig fig.)

      b) 5678.45 (6 sig fig.)

      c) 222 (3 sig fig.)

    ii. *Leading zeros* are those that precede all of the nonzero digits and are not counted as significant.
  - a) 0.00022 (2 sig fig.)
  - b) 0.0235 (3 sig fig.)
  - c) 0.954 (3 sig fig.)

    iii. *Captive zeros* are those that fall between nonzero digits and are counted as significant.
  - a) 10056 (5 sig fig.)
  - b) 2301 (4 sig fig.)
  - c) 100004 (6 sig fig.)

    iv. *Trailing zeros* are those at the end of a number and are only significant if the number is written with a decimal point.
  - a) 100 (1 sig fig.)
  - b) 100. (3 sig fig.)
  - c) 100.000 (6 sig fig.)

    v. In scientific notation, the *10^x part of the number* is not counted as significant.
  - a) 1.2×10^5 (2 sig fig.)
  - b) 2.33×10^3 (3 sig fig.)
  - c) 1.2004×10^{-3} (5 sig fig.)

    vi. *Exact numbers* have an unlimited number of significant figures. Exact numbers are those determined as a result of counting or by definition, e.g., 3 apples or 1.000 kg = 2.205 lb.

2. Following is a description of significant figures in math operations.

    i. When multiplying or dividing, limit the answer to the same number of significant figures that appear in the original data with the fewest number of significant figures.
  - a) $2.34 \div 1.34 = 1.75$ (rounded to 3 sig fig.)
  - b) $123 \times 6 = 700$ (rounded to 1 sig fig.)
  - c) $23 \div 34 = 0.68$ (rounded to 2 sig fig.)

    ii. When adding or subtracting, limit the answer to the same number of decimal places that appear in the original data with the fewest number of decimal places.
  - a) $57.3 + 12.6 = 69.9$
  - b) $7.0 + 3.22 = 10.2$
  - c) $11.3 - 6.66 = 4.6$

B. ACCURACY AND PRECISION

1. *Accuracy* is how close a measurement is to the real value.
2. *Precision* is how close a series of measurements are to one another.

C. WEIGHING

1. Allow cooling before weighing recently heated items, because convection currents may disturb the balance and hot items may damage a delicate electronic balance.
2. Use weighing boats to avoid damaging the pan of the balance with corrosive chemicals.

D. TITRATIONS

1. Rinse pipets and burets with the solution that they will contain during the titration, not water (to avoid diluting the solution).
2. Read the bottom of the meniscus.
3. Record one uncertain figure, but no more. In burets that are graduated to a tenth of a milliliter, then the final digit (second decimal place) should be recorded as either a "0" or a "5." Use "0" if the meniscus is directly ON a graduation, or "5" if it falls between two graduations. For example, if the meniscus falls between 23.40 and 23.50, record 23.45.

 III. PROCEDURES

A. METHODS OF SEPARATION

1. *Filtration* is the process of using a filter paper to separate an insoluble solid from a solution or liquid, such as filtering a precipitate from a solution.
2. *Distillation* is the process of heating a mixture of liquids, and relying upon the difference in boiling point to collect one (the lower boiling point component) above the other, such as distillation of ethanol (boiling point 78°C) and water (boiling point 100°C).

3. *Paper chromatography* is the process of separation of components based upon their relative affinities for a stationary phase (paper) and a moving phase (a solvent).

   i. R_f values are calculated by applying the following formula:

$$R_f = \frac{\text{distance traveled by comonent of mixture}}{\text{distance traveled by solvent front}}$$

IV. SAFETY

A. SAFETY RULES

1. Wear protective gear (goggles, aprons, gloves, etc.).
2. Use a fume hood when appropriate (with volatile chemicals).
3. Dilute acids by adding acid to water, not by adding water to acids.
4. Take care not to cross-contaminate chemicals.
5. Volatile and flammable substances should be heated using a water bath, not a naked flame.
6. Heat materials gently and point test tubes away from people.
7. Know the location of, and how to use, safety equipment.

V. DATA ANALYSIS, GRAPHS, AND INTERPRETATION

A. ERRORS

1. Minimize by repeating experiments and measurements and averaging the results.
2. Percentage error can be calculated by applying the following formula:

$$\% \text{ Error} = \frac{\left|\text{Experimental value} - \text{Actual value}\right|}{\text{Actual value}} \times 100$$

B. GRAPHING

1. Place the *independent variable* (the variable you have control over and are changing) on the *x* axis, and the *dependent variable* (the variable you are measuring and is changing as a result of changing the independent variable) on the *y* axis.

> *The contents of this chapter should be viewed as general laboratory knowledge and good practice when handling chemicals and data from experiments. They should be things that you have picked up from the lab component of your course. If you have taken a course with no lab component, or one where labs are not emphasized, you should study this chapter in more detail.*

INDEX

Notes

Notes

Notes

Notes

Notes

Notes

Notes

Notes

Notes

Notes